Therapeutic Relationships

Therapeutic Relationships

The Tripartite Model: Development and Applications to Family Systems Theory

John F. Butler, PhD

ROWMAN & LITTLEFIELD
Lanham • Boulder • New York • London

Published by Rowman & Littlefield
A wholly owned subsidiary of The Rowman & Littlefield Publishing Group, Inc.
4501 Forbes Boulevard, Suite 200, Lanham, Maryland 20706
www.rowman.com

Unit A, Whitacre Mews, 26-34 Stannary Street, London SE11 4AB

British Library Cataloguing in Publication Information Available

Library of Congress Cataloging-in-Publication Data Available

ISBN: 978-1-4422-5452-7 (cloth: alk. paper)
ISBN: 978-1-4422-5454-1 (pbk.: alk. paper)
ISBN: 978-1-4422-5453-4 (electronic)

♾™ The paper used in this publication meets the minimum requirements of American
National Standard for Information Sciences—Permanence of Paper for Printed Library
Materials, ANSI/NISO Z39.48-1992.

Printed in the United States of America

Dedicated to:

Murray Bowen, MD
1913–1990

William Meissner, SJ, MD
1931–2011

&

Charles Gelso, PhD

Contents

Preface

Freud's seminal paper, *The Dynamics of Transference*, continues in importance long after its publication (Freud, 1912). It is recognized that Freud discovered the concept of the transference. With this discovery, "the existence of a third figure" in the consultation room was recognized (Chertok, 1968, p. 566). A common element of all psychotherapy methods is the recognition of the importance of the therapeutic relationship and the interaction with outcome. Indeed, initiating and maintaining some degree of therapeutic connection is a basic feature of all psychotherapy models. While Freud was the first practitioner to write about the therapeutic relationship and the concept of transference, interest in this area extends beyond psychoanalytic psychotherapy. Today, publications continue with great regularity about the therapeutic relationship across the spectrum of methods of psychotherapy.

In the past several years, two individuals have written extensively about the therapeutic relationship in psychotherapy. One is William Meissner's writing several articles (Meissner, 1992, 1996a, 1998, 1999, 2000, 2006a, 2006b, 2007) and a book (Meissner, 1996b). The second is Charles Gelso and his colleagues (Gelso, 2014; Gelso & Samstag, 2008). Both Meissner and Gelso and his colleagues wrote about three distinct components of the therapeutic relationship (i.e., the alliance, transference/countertransference, and the real relationship). Meissner (2000) initially termed these three aspects *triune* (Meissner, 2000) and later a *tripartite model* (Meissner, 2007), whereas Gelso and Samstag referred to these three aspects as the "tripartite model" of the therapeutic relationship (Gelso, 2014; Gelso & Samstag, 2008). Since the term *tripartite* appears most often in the literature, that term is used in this book.

In a 2007 article, Meissner outlined the three important aspects existing in therapeutic relationships based primarily on psychoanalytic psychotherapy:

> In an attempt to bring a greater degree of clarity to the concept of the therapeutic alliance and broaden the scope of its application, I have reformulated the concept to include all those factors and dimensions of the analytic relation that constitute the therapeutic pact and determine the context within which the effective therapeutic interventions, interactions, and interpretative communication can take place. The tripartite composition of the analytic relation is the primary context for understanding alliance.
>
> As such, the alliance takes its place along with transference-countertransference and the real relation as the constitutive components or aspects of the analytic or therapeutic relation. These components are constantly intermingling and interacting in the analytic process, continually active in shaping and determining the patterns or relating and interacting between analyst and patient. (p. 231)

While Meissner's chief interest was in psychoanalytic psychotherapy, he nonetheless stressed the importance of these three elements of the therapeutic relationship: the alliance, transference, and counter-transference and the real relationship being present to one degree or another in all psychotherapies (Meissner, 2006a). There is an early connection between Dr. Bowen, a pioneer in family psychotherapy, and Dr. Meissner. That is, during his time at Georgetown as a Jesuit priest before he attended Harvard Medical School, Dr. Meissner worked with Dr. Bowen, completing multigenerational histories on several families. In addition, one of Dr. Meissner's earliest articles in his prolific writing career was on psychiatric aspects of the family (Meissner, 1964).

OVERALL PURPOSE

This book focuses on the development of the tripartite model of the therapeutic relationship and the origins and current status of the therapeutic role implied by the practice of family psychotherapy based on Bowen family systems theory. Family psychotherapy based on Bowen family systems theory rests on the concept of the family as an emotional unit. With this concept, the treatment focuses on the family unit not on a member with emotional symptoms. This concept remains important in Bowen family systems theory, where the orientation to the family unit places the therapeutic relationship in a broader perspective (Bowen, 1978, 2013). That is, a broader view is implied when the focus is on the family emotional unit regardless of who is in the consulting room.

It was during Bowen's Family Study Project, which will be discussed in detail in subsequent chapters, a fundamental change that advocated the nature of the therapeutic relationship was discussed. In early papers, Bowen viewed this new type of therapeutic relationship in two ways: "to be helpful while staying detached from the other person's immaturities. To be helpful with a problem without becoming responsible for the problem" (Bowen, 2013, p. 54). Later, Bowen (1978) saw this therapeutic relationship as emotionally connecting to family members but not getting caught in their emotionality. He termed this *emotional nonparticipation.* This refers to a therapeutic position of mastery of one's emotional overinvolvement with family members, the ability to emotionally connect with people, and use the concept of the family as an emotional unit as a guide. It does not mean the therapist is uncaring and distant.

Then and now this approach is unique compared to other psychotherapy models. Today the term *emotional neutrality,,* defined as the therapist's ability to manage his/her own reactivity and make emotional connections with family members, has replaced emotional nonparticipation. In family psychotherapy, reducing therapist's emotional reactions while working with family members is one challenge Bowen successfully managed during his research. Another goal of family psychotherapy is the analysis of emotional processes and patterns within families rather than the analysis of a transference relationship (Bowen, 2013).

Bowen's therapeutic position is different from, and in fact the opposite of, a traditional emphasis on the therapeutic alliance between a therapist and a patient. Instead of encouraging the intensity of the therapeutic alliance, Bowen worked on discouraging those behaviors that would intensify the alliance (Bowen, 1978). The rationale for this position was threefold: The focus was on the family unit and not on an individual; most therapists are not trained to manage high levels of emotional intensity; and, specifically, Bowen thought the emotionality should be redirected to the patient's family rather than to the therapeutic alliance. Following the Family Study Project, Bowen extended this therapeutic role with individuals, couples, and families.

What degree of training is necessary to effectively manage high degrees of emotionality in clinical practice? For psychoanalytic psychotherapy it remains personal analysis; for Bowen's theory it is ongoing formal study of family systems theory, personal coaching, and using differentiation of self for self-management. The formal study of theory means several years of association with the Bowen Center for the Study of the Family or other related training programs for postgraduate training in family systems theory. A therapist cannot achieve mastery of family systems theory by simply reading a book or by attending a workshop.

While Bowen never discussed the triadic nature of the therapeutic relationship, he did note two aspects of this concept. First, he commented on the therapeutic alliance: "The alliance is at the core of the therapeutic relationship, the main treatment modality of relationship therapy" (Bowen, 1978, p. 191). Intensifying a therapeutic relationship fosters an alliance (Bowen, 1978). In early papers about the Family Study, Bowen (2013) also wrote about the importance of the concepts of transference and countertransference. There were also comments about these concepts in his classic, *Family Therapy in Clinical Practice* (Bowen, 1978). In fact, although inherent to Bowen's theory are the concepts of transference and countertransference, a different conceptual base was proposed, that is, the concept of the emotional system replaced with the concept of the unconscious.

The triadic model of the therapeutic relationship provides a benchmark on important interactive components applying to all methods of psychotherapy. The model is also a useful yardstick to compare and contrast psychotherapy methods. In one sense, Bowen alluded to the alliance and transference and countertransference concepts to help distinguish his method from conventional psychotherapy and family therapy. Bowen concluded that his approach was so different that he suggested terms such as *coaching* or *supervising* to describe the process (Bowen, 1978). Bowen did his best to distance himself from the term *therapeutic relationship* due to the connotations with the usual meanings (M. Kerr, personal communication, 2009). *Coaching* is a different process than a *therapeutic alliance*. A challenge today is that the term *coaching* has a different meaning than what Bowen intended. Today, coaching often refers to executive or personal coaching rather than a therapeutic role.

Among students of Bowen's theory there is diversity of thinking about the therapeutic relationship. For example, the Emeritus Director of the Bowen Center for the Family avoids the use of the term *therapeutic relationship* in favor of the term *consultation* with the family (M. Kerr, personal communication, 2013). Another senior faculty member of the Bowen Center is sensitive to the term *therapeutic relationship* because of its usual connotations. He views coaching in family psychotherapy as very different from the typical therapeutic role (D. Papero, personal communication, 2013).

OVERVIEW OF UPCOMING CHAPTERS

This book is about therapeutic relationships, a universal aspect in all helping relationships. Whether one is a physician in a general or a specialty medical practice, a nurse practitioner or physician assistant in family practice, a nurse practitioner in a mental health setting, or a therapist in a mental health clinic, the nuances of therapeutic relationships are ever present. However, the degree of emotional intensity in these relationships varies by the type of activity. This book, however, focuses on those therapeutic relationships present in individual, marital, or family psychotherapy.

Furthermore, the book discusses Bowen's thinking about the nature of the therapeutic relationship and how it differs from conventional psychoanalytic psychotherapy developed during the NIMH Family Study Project. Detailed observations about the origin and evolution of the therapeutic relationship are now possible because of the recent publication of Bowen's original papers from his archives at the History of Medicine Division of the National Library of Medicine (Bowen, 2013). His original papers now supplement his early writings so familiar to many in his book *Family Therapy in Clinical Practice.*

Part 1 of this volume is an introduction and highlights the findings of meta-analytic research on the importance of the therapeutic relationship on outcome in psychotherapy. Part 2 highlights the work of the two most important contributors in the development of the tripartite model of the therapeutic relationship—William Meissner and Charles Gelso. Part 3 explores the origins and development of family psychotherapy and coaching in family systems theory and practice. This includes chapters on the evolution of the therapeutic relationship in Bowen family systems theory, including historical development, importance of the concept of the family as an emotional unit, the distinctive features of a coaching relationship in family systems theory, and an application of the triadic model to Bowen family systems theory. Finally, part 4 presents the distinctive features of family psychotherapy and coaching in Bowen family systems theory.

Some overall questions for readers of this book are as follows: (a) What is the particular theoretical orientation behind your clinical work? (b) How does your theory guide your approach to your therapeutic relationship? (c) What is your thinking about three components of therapeutic relationships (i.e., alliance, transference/countertransference, real relationship)? (d) How do these components operate in your practice and which is the most prominent and why?

Acknowledgments

I acknowledge the long-standing work of Catherine Rakow, formerly of the Pittsburg Family Center, on the Bowen Archives. Her efforts guided my research on the Bowen Archives, now housed at the History of Medicine Division of the Library of Medicine. I am also grateful to the editorial board of the journal *Family Systems* from the Bowen Center of the Study of the Family for permission to adapt two of my papers published in that journal for this book.

This book is dedicated to the three people directly responsible for publishing it: first, to William Meissner, SJ, MD, for his many publications about the triadic model of the therapeutic relationship. His book, *The Therapeutic Alliance*, a comprehensive review of the alliance and its components, was my initial guide in this area. It was Dr. Meissner's writings and my research in the Bowen Archives that formed the basis of this book. Second, I am indebted to Charles Gelso, PhD, who recently retired from the University of Maryland, and his many students for their work to operationalize the components of the therapeutic relationship and their research on these components. Third, although I never personally met Dr. Bowen, I have seen and heard him in countless videos and audio tapes and read most of his unpublished and published writings. I have done my best to accurately represent family systems theory. If I have failed in any way to do so, the fault is mine, not the theory's.

Part One

Chapter One

Introduction and Overview

In 2012 we celebrated the 100th anniversary of Freud's seminal paper, *The Dynamics of Transference* (Freud, 1912). One major contribution of this paper was the recognition of the importance of the emotional nature of the doctor–patient relationship (Chertok, 1968). He noted, "the affective nature of the doctor-patient relationship was perceived from the very earliest days of psychotherapy" (p. 560). Chertok (1968) credits Freud as the first practitioner to write and teach about the therapeutic relationship and the concept of transference. The seminal concept of the therapeutic relationship extended beyond psychoanalytic theory and practice, and this practice remains an important area of interest in individual psychotherapy and marriage and family therapy. Interest in the area of the therapeutic relationship is demonstrated by the number of research articles on this topic between 1950 and 2010. Horvath (2013) documented about 9,500 articles in the areas of transference, the alliance, and the facilitative conditions of the therapist. Indeed, a common thread of all psychotherapies, including individual, group, marriage, or family, is the acknowledgment of the importance of the therapeutic relationship.

Marriage and family therapy adopted the idea of the therapeutic relationship from psychoanalysis and individual psychotherapy and applied this concept to work with couples and families. However, new concepts, such as split and intact alliances, were developed based on working with more than one person. In addition, marriage and family therapy currently emphasizes designing and implementing ways to measure the therapeutic alliance.

Just what is the therapeutic relationship? What does it include? What are the specific components? Are there differences based on theoretical orientation? Are there commonalities in the therapeutic relationship across theoretical orientations? For people involved in the various helping professions, including clinical social workers, psychologists, psychiatrists, counselors, and nurse practitioners, these are important questions. This chapter has several purposes. First, due to the continued importance and emphasis on the topic of the therapeutic relationship and outcome in psychotherapy, meta-analytic studies in this area are reviewed. Second, seminal contributors to the tripartite model of the therapeutic relationship are evaluated. Third, family systems theory's perspective on the therapeutic relationship is highlighted.

META-ANALYTIC REVIEWS AND THE THERAPEUTIC RELATIONSHIP

Meta-analysis has become an important tool in the area of evaluation research in many subjects. For our purposes, there have been several meta-analytic reviews on the therapeutic relationship and outcome. It is the purpose of this next section to chronologically review these meta-analytic studies on the therapeutic relationship and outcome in psychotherapy.

A robust relationship has been found between a positive therapeutic relationship and therapy outcome (Horvath, 2006). Horvath and Symonds (1991) published the first meta-analysis on the relationship between the working alliance and psychotherapy outcome. They comment that "the influence of the therapist-client relationship on the outcome of psychotherapy is one of the oldest themes in therapy research" (p. 138). Horvath and Symonds (1991) used 24 studies comprising 20 data sets for their meta-analysis. With this sample they found the effect size (ES) between the working alliance and outcome in therapy as 0.26. They found the "working alliance a relatively robust variable linking therapy process to outcome" (p. 146).

Martin, Garske, and Davis (2000) published the next meta-analysis review of 20 years of research. They reviewed the most often used alliance measures across 58 published and 21 unpublished studies. The result was a correlation of 0.22, which they concluded indicated a moderate relationship to outcome. They also found "that alliance is moderately related to outcome" (p. 446). Last, the alliance measures were found to have acceptable reliability, and, thus, no additional new measures of the working alliance were recommended. The researchers recommend the Working Alliance Inventory as acceptable for research efforts.

Horvath (2001) provided the next meta-analytic study, examining data from two past meta-analyses (i.e., Horvath & Symonds, 1991; Martin et al., 2000) in addition to 10 recent investigations between 1997 and 2000 that totaled 90 studies. "An analysis of the relation between alliance and therapy outcome of this data yielded a weighted mean overall ES of .21" (p. 366). Horvath (2001) concludes: "It is likely that a little over half of the beneficial effect of psychotherapy accounted for in previous meta-analyses are linked to the quality of the alliance" (p. 366).

Horvath, Fluckiger, and Symonds (2011) recently reviewed the alliance in individual psychotherapy. Theirs was the fourth meta-analysis since the early 1990s that focused on the relationship between psychotherapy outcome and the alliance. Horvath et al. (2011) examined 158 published and 53 unpublished studies covering 14,000 treatments. In terms of their results the aggregate ES was 0.275, which is consistent with past meta-analytic studies. They conclude that the results "are moderate but highly reliable" (p. 11).

In addition to meta-analytic reviews about the alliance in individual psychotherapy, Friedlander, Escudero, Heatherington, and Diamond (2011) examined the alliance in couple and family therapy. Their meta-analytic review of this area examined 24 studies and found an overall weighted average ES of $r = 0.26$; in family therapy in 17 studies the ES was $r = 0.24$; and with the 17 couple studies the ES was $r = 0.37$.

Shirk, Karver, and Brown (2011) reviewed meta-analytic studies in the area of child and adolescent psychotherapy. They reviewed 16 studies with 658 youth with a resulting ES of 0.22 and concluded that the alliance of all family members is predictive of outcome.

In an interesting study about managing countertransference, Hayes, Gelso, and Hummel (2011) summarized 22 meta-analytic studies along with 5 dissertations in this area and located 10 studies in the area of countertransference and psychotherapy outcome. The ES was –0.16 with a sample size of 769 patients. Countertransference was inversely related to outcome in psychotherapy. Hayes et al. (2011) also investigated the question of countertransference management in reducing the effects of countertransference. As many as 11 quantitative studies resulted in an ES of –0.14 with 1,065 participants. Finally, with the question whether countertransference management improves psychotherapy outcome, the ES was 0.56 across 478 patients.

Whereas the relationship between outcome in psychotherapy and the therapeutic alliance is modest, this association has been shown as robust over many meta-analytic studies over the past 20 years (Fluckiger, Del Rey, Wampold, & Symonds, 2012). However, this modest relationship has been found to account for only 7 percent of the variance (see Fluckiger et al. 2012).

Given this review of the meta-analytic studies, it is useful to have a yardstick to examine effect sizes in general and specifically to compare the results for the therapeutic alliance with other areas. For example, how do the meta-analytic studies in the alliance and psychotherapy outcome compare to meta-analytic studies in psychotherapy in general and specifically with the area of antidepressant medications? Shedler (2010) fortunately provides such an article in *The Efficacy of Psychodynamic Psychotherapy*. Shedler (2010) reminds readers that an effect size (ES) of 1.0 indicates that the treated patient is 1 standard deviation (SD) more improved than an untreated patient. Furthermore, quoting Cohen (1988), who authored one of the earliest texts on meta-analysis, Shedler (2010) concluded that an ES of 0.8 or larger is large, 0.5 is moderate, and the ES of 0.2 is found to be small.

Shedler (2010) next examines meta-analytic studies involving psychotherapy outcome. The first meta-analysis done by Smith, Glass, and Miller (1980) covering 475 studies produced an ES of 0.85 for patients receiving treatment versus untreated controls. Robinson, Berman, and Neimeyer (1990) reported on 37 psychotherapy studies on the treatment of depression with an overall ES of 0.73. All these are moderate-to-large ESs.

For another comparison, Shedler (2010) provides ESs for a variety of antidepressant medications. They are as follows: Prozac, 0.26; Zoloft, 0.26; Celexa, 0.24; Lexapro, 0.31; and Cymbalta, 0.30. The introduction to Shedler's (2010) article provides a useful benchmark for comparisons of the meta-analytic studies involving the alliance and outcome in psychotherapy.

By way of a summary, Horvath (2013) highlights the changes in psychotherapy outcome research across 50 years following Strupp's famous 1963 article, by finding that the meta-analytic studies of the alliance/outcome association have been very consistent; there is a modest but very reliable relationship between therapy outcome and the alliance. This result seems to hold regardless of the source of the ratings, type of treatment, or clinical problem. These meta-analyses result from 200 independent research studies involving over 18,000 treatments.

THE TRIPARTITE MODEL OF THE THERAPEUTIC RELATIONSHIP: SEMINAL CONTRIBUTORS

It is difficult to discuss the history and current status of efforts to achieve conceptual clarity about the therapeutic relationship without first acknowledging that the concept of the therapeutic relationship has undergone considerable evolution since Freud's initial writings. The history of the therapeutic relationship is long and complex, with many agreements and disagreements about its nature and components. Does the therapeutic relationship only include transference and countertransference, or are there other aspects? Although it would be worthwhile, it is far beyond the scope of this section to review the history of this concept. It is the purpose of this section to review the history and development of just the tripartite model of the therapeutic relationship.

The history and present status of work on a tripartite model of the therapeutic relationship are intertwined with the history of the concept of the therapeutic relationship itself. Actually, many articles about the therapeutic relationship begin with a brief history of the concept. For example, Safran and Muran (2000) provide a concise history of the therapeutic alliance, and

Friedlander, Valentin, and Heatherington (2006) review this concept in their focus on System for Observing Family Therapy Alliances (SOFTA).

Even though the therapeutic relationship has enjoyed a long history and evolution, according to Meissner (2006a), there has been a "lack of conceptual clarity" (p. 265) about the therapeutic relationship. However, several individuals have made seminal contributions toward specifying the critical elements involved in therapeutic relationships. Attention will now be directed to chronologically highlighting these contributions.

SIGMUND FREUD (1856–1939)

It is universally recognized that any discussion of the therapeutic relationship must begin with Sigmund Freud. Freud is inarguably recognized as the person who developed a coherent theory and method of practice based on the importance of the therapeutic relationship.

It would be inaccurate to assume that Freud viewed the therapeutic relationship as only including transference and countertransference. For example, in his own writings he discusses the importance of establishing rapport with patients (Freud, 1912/1958). In addition, Freud viewed the patient as a "collaborator" (Freud, 1912/1958). Freud also found the formulation of an analytic pact extremely important in the conduct of analysis. Greenson (1967) views Freud's writings as an early description of the working alliance when Freud remarked "make no interpretations to the patient until a rapport has been developed" (p. 165).

ELIZABETH ZETZEL (1907–1970)

In her classic article, *The Current Concept of the Transference*, Zetzel wrote about "a modification of analytic technique" (p. 121). That is, she sought to distinguish the therapeutic alliance from the transference neurosis. It was Zetzel who introduced the term *therapeutic alliance*. She concluded, "effective analysis depends on a sound therapeutic alliance, a prerequisite for which is the existence, before analysis, of a degree of mature ego functions" (p. 370).

RALPH R. GREENSON (1911–1979)

Greenson expanded Zetzel's concept of the therapeutic alliance and expanded its components. His work on specifying the nature of the therapeutic alliance has formed the basis for the writings of future generations of clinicians and researchers in this area. Greenson was the first to describe the tripartite nature of the therapeutic relationship that included the alliance, transference and countertransference, and the real relationship. Greenson's 1967 book *The Technique and Practice of Psychoanalysis*, Volume 1, provides details about the concept of the working alliance. He defined the working alliance as "the relatively non-neurotic, rational relationship between patient and analyst which makes it possible for the patient to work purposely in the analytic situation" (Greenson, 1967, p. 46).

Harris (2005) summarized Greenson's contributions toward clarifying the components of the therapeutic relationship as follows:

> Greenson goes to distinguish and hold separate places for a working alliance and real relationship. The working alliance encompasses many elements: continuity, commitment, ways of being within the hour, and management of time and money—elements that we would think of as aspects of the frame. (p. 204)

Greenson, in discussing the real relationship as distinct from matters that deepen or hold the therapeutic alliance, speaks about genuineness (including straightforward admission of errors) and an orientation to reality, as well as an appreciation of the extra-analytic reality of the analyst (e.g., family, frailties, contexts). He sees the working alliance as a permanent aspect of an analysis and the emergence of a real relationship as an aspect of the later stages of analysis (p. 204).

Surveying the literature since Freud, Greenson (1967) concluded that the history of the therapeutic relationship recognized that there was more to the relationship than just transference reactions. Greenson's major accomplishment was to define the tripartite model that included transference reactions, the working alliance, and the real relationship. "These three models of relating to the analyst are interrelated. They influence one another, blend into one another, and can cover one another" (Greenson, 1967, p. 219).

EDWARD S. BORDIN (1913–1992)

In the late 1970s Bordin authored an article entitled, *The Generalizability of the Psychoanalytic Concept of the Working Alliance*. While not recognizing a tripartite model of the therapeutic relationship like Greenson had, Bordin used the term *working alliance* instead of *therapeutic relationship*. While Bordin is not usually identified with the tripartite model of the therapeutic relationship, his paper with his own tripartite model became very influential in specifying elements of the therapeutic or working alliance and in influencing future research on the alliance.

Bordin (1979) attempted to merge two theoretical traditions: first from Sterba (1934) and Menninger (1958), and second, from Zetzel (1956) and

Greenson (1967). "Fusing these contributions, we can speak of the working alliance as including three features: an agreement of goals, an assignment of tasks or a series of tasks, and the development of bonds" (p. 253). Bordin (1979) viewed these three features as operating to some degree in all psychotherapies. Bordin's seminal contribution lies in the significant and lasting influence his tripartite conceptualization has had on research on the therapeutic alliance and the development of measurement instruments. His general formulation of goals, tasks, and bonds as a part of all psychotherapy later formed the basis for the Working Alliance Inventory (WAI), one of the primary research and clinical instruments on the working alliance.

CHARLES J. GELSO (1941–PRESENT) AND JEAN CARTER (1951–PRESENT)

In 1985, Gelso and Carter authored a significant paper on the therapeutic relationship in psychotherapy and counseling.

Their article is in two parts. Part 1 focuses on the therapeutic relationship and builds directly on Greenson's classic proposal that "all relationships in counseling and therapy more or less consist of three interrelated components—a working alliance, a transference configuration, and a real relationship" (Gelso & Carter, 1985, p. 157). The second part outlines how perspectives about the therapeutic relationship differ according to theoretical perspectives. The first part of their article is an excellent review of the tripartite perspective of the therapeutic relationship. Each component, the working alliance, transference and countertransference, and the real relationship are reviewed in detail. They conclude:

> We would take Greenson's thinking a step further and propose that all therapeutic relationships consist of these three components, although the salience and important of each part during counseling or therapy will vary according to the theoretical perspective of the therapist and the particulars of a given therapy. (Gelso & Carter, 1986, p. 161)

Influenced by the humanistic school, Gelso and Carter's seminal contribution toward an understanding of the therapeutic relationship is a focus on the aspect of the real relationship. They believe that the real relationship has been the most neglected aspect of the tripartite conceptualization of the therapeutic relationship (Gelso & Carter, 1994). Gelso and Carter (1994) further note that the real relationship has two features—genuineness and realistic perception. Gelso and his colleagues also developed the Real Relationship Inventory with different versions for clients and therapists.

W. W. MEISSNER, SJ (1931–2010)

Meissner wore two distinct hats in his life; he was both a Jesuit priest and a psychiatrist. He was associated with Boston College and the Boston Psychoanalytic Institute. While a student at Georgetown University, he worked on multigenerational family histories in consultation with Murray Bowen. In 1964, Meissner's first paper was a review of psychiatric aspects of the family.

Meissner published many books and articles on the components of the therapeutic relationship. One of his basic assumptions is that there has been a lack of clarity among the elements of the therapeutic relationship (2006). Like authors before him in this area, he also builds upon the work of Zetzel (1956) and Greenson (1965). Meissner assumes that that the elements of the therapeutic relationship can in fact be distinguished. Although these elements might be defined differently, Meissner finds the therapeutic relationship having "three discriminable components that can be distinguished and occur simultaneously, concurrently, and in varying degrees of intermingling" (2006, p. 265). Following Greenson, Meissner sees these as the therapeutic alliance, transferences and countertransferences, and the real relationship.

Meissner (2006) defines the alliance as a therapeutic pact that determines the context for therapeutic interventions. Transference and countertransference "provide the material on which the psychoanalytic process works," and the real relationship includes other aspects "that reflects their existence and status as real persons functioning in the real world" (p. 265). Meissner also found that there is a positive relationship between the therapeutic alliance and therapeutic outcome.

As with other writers in this area, Meissner finds the following:

> The therapeutic relationship, as I have implied, in fact involves three compo-
> nents that can occur simultaneously with the therapeutic relationship but can
> be adequately distinguished. These components are the therapeutic alliance,
> transference and real relationship. (1996, p. 17)

FAMILY PSYCHOTHERAPY AND MURRAY BOWEN—THE THERAPEUTIC RELATIONSHIP IN A BROADER PERSPECTIVE

Murray Bowen's psychiatric training began at the Menninger Foundation in Topeka, Kansas, from 1946 to 1954 and was based on Freudian theory, the predominate model at that time, where a focus on the therapeutic relationship was critical. It was during his tenure at Menninger's, first in training and later as a staff member, that Bowen began his transition away from conventional psychoanalytic theory.

Bowen left the Menninger Foundation in 1954 and began a historic family-oriented research program in the National Institutes of Mental Health (NIMH) at Bethesda, Maryland. The research program, the 3-East Family Study Program, initially involved hospitalizing mother–child dyads for the purpose of observation and study of symbiosis in families; all children were diagnosed with schizophrenia. Bowen's interest in psychological symbiosis had actually begun during his training and subsequent clinical practice at Menninger's (Kerr & Bowen, 1988). Bowen was interested in how symbiosis functions among family members. He determined that "symbiosis is transferable, observable by others and treatable. It takes participation of both to sustain it" (Rakow, 2007, p. 13). At first, traditional psychoanalytic treatment methods were used with the mothers and their daughters. That is, each was seen in individual psychoanalytic therapy. Three mother–daughter dyads were observed and studied during the first year of the project. Even though there were initially only three family units, dealing 24/7 with their high levels of emotional intensity proved to be a formidable challenge for all staff. These families were experts in inviting staff overinvolvement.

For the last three years of the project, a significant change was made in the direction of the research; fathers and nonsymptomatic siblings were also hospitalized in addition to the mothers and the schizophrenic child. This shift was based on the emerging concept of the family as an emotional unit. The family-as-an-emotional-unit concept expresses the emotional reciprocity existing within the family. Using a larger lens to conceptualize the family as an emotional unit, the mother–daughter pairs studied during the first year of the project were then seen as a part of a larger emotional system involving the entire family.

This new orientation was foreign to a mental health world accustomed to a focus on the individual. In some ways, it still is today. The concept of the family as an emotional unit, the central finding of the revised Family Study Project, began a new theoretical and clinical direction that continues today. If the lens of treatment is on the family as an emotional unit with an individual who may have emotional symptoms, then the treatment should be directed to the family unit. However, there was no existing model for treating families in this manner.

Based on theory at that time involving the psychological symbiosis between parents and their children and direct observation, Bowen and his colleagues derived a new and innovative method of working with families called family psychotherapy. Family psychotherapy began literally in daily patient–staff groups where several family units, including parents, the symptomatic child, and a nonsymptomatic sibling, met with staff members. These groups greatly assisted in the ongoing efforts of managing staff overinvolvement with family members and helped to reduce anxiety and symptoms in the families.

The family psychotherapy method, initiated during the Family Study Project, transformed the therapeutic relationship in several areas. First, the therapist tried to achieve a balanced position, striving to achieve a neutral position with the family members while working to maintain emotional connections with all family members. Second, the therapist tried to resolve a common therapeutic dilemma by working to avoid psychologically replacing the parents. Third, parents were also asked to shoulder more responsibility for their child in the hospital instead of turning over complete care to hospital staff. Last, a new goal for family psychotherapy was introduced. The purpose became the observation of intense family processes rather than the traditional therapeutic role of the enhancement and interpretation of a transference relationship.

Based on the concept of the family as an emotional unit, Bowen concluded the therapeutic relationship must be centered on the family. This change involved a new orientation that included viewing the family as supportive and helpful to the patient rather than toxic (Rakow, 2007). In *Family Therapy in Clinical Practice*, a classic work among of his most important published papers, Bowen explicated the development of his innovative views about the therapeutic relationship with families as well as couples and individuals. In fact, part of the title of this book, *The Therapeutic Relationship in Broader Perspective*, is taken from a section in his book where he addresses the contribution that his family research made toward a new understanding of the therapeutic relationship and how this differs from traditional family therapy.

Bowen noted that when a therapist begins working with a family, the family is changed, with the result that there are both positive and negative implications. The role assumed by the therapist is critical; are they an expert or coach? Bowen sought to minimize his position as a psychiatrist. The focus of assessment and treatment should be on the nuclear and extended families of the identified patient, not just the identified patient. This approach is in contrast to the traditional view where the principal focus is on evaluating the identified patient (IP); the nuclear and extended families are largely ignored. Assessment of only the IP is viewed by family systems theory as incomplete.

It is difficult to convey in a few short introductory comments the importance and implications of this transformative event in the theory and practice of family psychotherapy. Bowen and his colleagues were initially trained in the theory and practice of psychoanalytic theory and practice. Their shift from this traditional psychoanalytic perspective to one centered on the family as an emotional unit was both a challenge and a remarkable accomplishment. This new model was grounded in the family-as-a-unit theory and based on daily observation and intensive work with a small number of families over several years. Bowen and his colleagues began a variation of single-case experimental designs long before they became fashionable.

While Bowen did not advocate the typical tripartite model of the therapeutic relationship as outlined by Greenson and Meissner, he did not exclude the concepts of transference and countertransference from family systems theory. During the Family Study Project Bowen and his colleagues diligently worked to *minimize* or *dilute* transference problems with the families. While Bowen recognized the validity of these concepts, he did not accept their theoretical underpinnings. The concepts of transference and countertransference are forever linked to psychoanalytic theory. Terms like *fusion* and *automatic reactivity* emerged in family systems theory to describe the process in a more neutral way and because they did not automatically imply psychoanalytic theory. Transference and countertransference are to Freud as triangles and differentiation are to Bowen. Later, Bowen would develop his eight interlocking theoretical concepts and apply his ideas about the therapeutic relationship originating with families to individuals and couples.

SUMMARY

A modest association between a positive therapeutic relationship and outcome in psychotherapy has been demonstrated over 20 years with several meta-analytic studies. Shedler (2010) provides a useful benchmark to compare these findings to other areas. The meta-analytic studies focusing on the therapeutic relationship and positive outcome compare favorably to other meta-analytic studies with tricyclic antidepressant medication but have smaller ESs than the meta-analytic studies on general psychotherapy outcome studies.

The tripartite model, which includes the components of the alliance, transference and countertransference, and the real relationship, was first established during the 1950s. The therapeutic relationship has always included more than just transference reactions; however, the tripartite model has not achieved universal acceptance.

Murray Bowen, an early pioneer in marriage and family therapy theory and practice, derived a much different conceptualization of the therapeutic relationship. From Bowen's perspective, the therapeutic relationship based on family systems theory is so different from the therapeutic relationship in other modalities that he used different terms such as *coaching* and *supervising* to more accurately describe the process.

Influenced by his NIMH Family Study Project, Bowen chartered a significantly different course from conventional practice by viewing the family as an emotional unit and by directing treatment to the family unit. Bowen's

innovative approach to the therapeutic relationship changes the basic therapeutic functions. In his view, the therapist must achieve a balance; they must
emotionally connect to the family members yet work to remain outside the
family's intensity. In addition, Bowen did not embrace the role of psychologically assuming a parental role with family members. He also retained the
concepts of transference and countertransference within his family systems
theory but rejected the psychoanalytic theory behind them.

Now that I have laid out the general progress of the therapeutic relationship in individual therapy to the tripartite model and its applicability to family psychotherapy development, I will go into more detail on the theoretical
contributions of two of the architects of the tripartite model, Charles Gelso
(in chapter 2) and William Meissner (in chapter 3).

Part Two

Chapter Two

The Contributions of Charles Gelso, PhD

While the early history of the therapeutic relationship includes names such as Freud, Sterba, Zetzel, and Greenson, for the past three decades two names stand out as making significant contributions to this important area. These are Charles Gelso and his colleagues and William Meissner. This chapter highlights the important and lasting impact of Charles Gelso and his colleagues in understanding the interactive components of the therapeutic relationship, including the alliance, transference and countertransference, and the real relationship.

Charles Gelso has individually and in collaboration with several of his colleagues for decades been clarifying, researching, and writing about components of the therapeutic relationship. Gelso and his colleague, Jean Carter, wrote their first paper on the therapeutic relationship in 1985. Theirs was a comprehensive review of the topic, and in fact the entire journal edition was devoted to their article. Gelso and Carter (1985) proposed this definition of the therapeutic relationship: "The relationship is the feelings and attitudes that counseling participants have toward one another, and the manner in which these are expressed" (p. 159). Gelso and Carter (1985) specified the three components of the therapeutic relationship, offered propositions about each, and in the second part of the article, showed how those components might apply to major clinical approaches.

In their initial article, Gelso and Carter (1985) discussed the three components of the therapeutic relationship, which include the alliance, transference and countertransference, and the real relationship. Later in a book chapter in 2008, Gelso and Carter (1985) proposed what was termed the *tripartite model* of the therapeutic relationship. They wrote,

> It is an understatement to say that there are many ways of framing the relationship that exists between a client and therapist in counseling and psychotherapy.

The frame that we have selected for the chapter divides the relationships into three interrelated components, a working alliance, a transference-countertransference configuration, and what may be termed a real relationship. The tripartite model, as it is formulated here, rests on the assumption that each and every psychotherapy relationship consists, to one degree or another, of a working alliance, a transference-countertransference configuration, and a real relationship. (p. 267)

MEISSNER AND GELSO

The second scholar who has made a major contribution to an understanding of the therapeutic relationship is William Meissner, MD. Writing primarily in the area of psychoanalytic theory and practice, he authored many books, book chapters, and articles in psychiatry and theology.

Meissner wrote that understanding the therapeutic relationship could be helped by conceptually separating it into three interacting aspects, including the alliance, transference and countertransference, and the real relationship. He termed this the "triune construction of the analytic relation" (Meissner, 2000, p. 513).

Both Gelso and Meissner developed the theoretical underpinnings of the broad concept of the therapeutic relationship into three conceptually separate but interactive components. They may have used different terms (i.e., triune, tripartite), but both emphasized how the therapeutic relationship could be better understood with this perspective. Gelso's most significant contribution was in researching the three components of the therapeutic relationship. Meissner (whom I will treat in more detail in chapter 3), who wrote from the perspective of psychoanalytic theory and practice, highlighted the nuances of the therapeutic relationship between the analyst and the analysand. Both provided important perspectives about this fundamental area of psychotherapy.

The title of this book follows Gelso's term *tripartite* aspects of the therapeutic relationship used in several of his articles and books. This term is utilized because it is already in the literature, and creating another term seems unnecessary and potentially confusing. The next sections highlight the important contributions of Gelso individually and with his colleagues by reviewing their seminal papers. My commentaries are provided after each section of contributions.

CONTRIBUTIONS OF CHARLES J. GELSO, PHD

Charles Gelso focused on theory and research on the therapeutic relationship from a counseling and clinical psychology perspective. His efforts now extend beyond counseling psychology to other mental health disciplines. Not only did Gelso introduce this topic to audiences outside of psychology, he also sought to operationally define the constructs of the therapeutic relationship and to generate important research about the components of the therapeutic relationship. His writing and research on the real relationship, one of the three constructs of the therapeutic relationship, is especially well known.

The work of Gelso and his colleagues builds on the foundation by Greenson (1967), who first wrote about the triadic aspects of the therapeutic relationship. Gelso and his colleagues worked to define the concepts of the therapeutic relationship, derive testable propositions, and compare major psychotherapy models using the tripartite model. In addition to individual papers, Gelso and Gelso and his colleagues have also authored several books. For example, in 1998, Gelso and Hayes completed *The Psychotherapy Relationship: Theory, Research and Practice*; in 2007 Gelso and Hayes authored *Countertransference and the Therapist's Inner Experience*; and finally in 2011, Gelso wrote *The Real Relationship in Psychotherapy: The Hidden Foundation of Change*. The following sections review book chapters and papers by Gelso and Gelso and his colleagues on conceptual and research aspects of the three important components of the therapeutic relationship.

SEMINAL BOOK CHAPTERS BY GELSO AND HIS COLLEAGUES

Gelso and Samtag (2008). A Tripartite Model of the Therapeutic Relationship

> It is an understatement to say that there are many ways of framing the relationship that exists between a client and therapist in counseling and psychotherapy. The frame that we have selected for this chapter divides the relationship into three interrelated components: a working alliance, a transference-countertransference configuration, and what may be termed a real relationship. (p. 267)

The authors begin their book chapter with the assumption that the tripartite model consisting of the working alliance, transference, and real relationship is present in every type of psychotherapy. They acknowledge the debt to psychoanalytic theory and practice for the origin of this perspective. The authors focus on this model in three areas. First, they propose definitions of each component of the tripartite model; second, theoretical matters and research findings are highlighted; and last, they discuss how the three components operate in practice. For this chapter, the authors use the definition of the therapeutic relationship proposed originally by Gelso and Carter (1985); *"the relationships may be seen as the feelings and attitudes the therapy participants have toward one another and the manner in which these are expressed"* (italics added, Gelso & Samstag, 2008, p. 268).

The authors make an importance observation concerning what the therapeutic relationship is *not*. They conclude that the therapeutic relationship is not the particular techniques utilized by a therapist based on a particular theoretical orientation.

Gelso and Samstag (2008) conclude that of the three components of the therapeutic relationship, it is the working alliance that is the most studied and researched. The authors note, however, that this term has a confusing history. That is, many terms have been used, including the *working alliance* by Greenson (1965), the *helping alliance* (Luborsky, 1976), and the *therapeutic alliance* (Zetzel, 1956). To clarify potential confusion about the term, they conclude the following:

> We prefer the label *working alliance* because it captures the importance of purposive and collaborative effort on the part of the client and the therapist—as distinct from the concept of the *therapeutic alliance*, which has been identified more specifically as the affective bond the client develops for the therapist. The term *therapeutic alliance* is problematic because it is too easily equated with the overall therapeutic relationship of general affective tone of the interactions and the concept then loses its unique theoretical value. (p. 269)

Reviewing the research on the working alliance, the authors summarize that positive outcome of treatment is related to a positive working alliance especially in the early sessions. Gelso and Samstag (2008) review Freud's perspective on the various types of transferences present in clinical practice and in other situations. Freud (1912/1958) wrote that transferences could be one of three types: positive, negative, and erotic. The authors used the classical perspective of this component because this helped distinguishing transferences from working alliances. In summary, "the quality that makes an experience transferential is that the client clings to the perception or experience of the therapist, failing to let go of it in the face of contrary evidence" (p. 271).

Related to the concept of transference is countertransference. The authors label this as a "double helix" (p. 273). That is, it can be seen as a negative influence that must be minimized for successful analysis, and at the same time recognition of this concept is a therapeutic necessity. Whereas there are several definitions of countertransference, the authors side with what they call "an integrative conception" (p. 274). Gelso and Samstag (2008) adopt Gelso and Hayes's (2007) definition of countertransference as "the therapist's internal and external reactions that are shaped by the therapist's past and present emotional conflicts and vulnerabilities" (p. 25).

Finally, the authors view the real relationship as "psychotherapy's hidden dimension" (p. 276). Of the three aspects of the therapeutic relationship, Gelso individually and in consultation with colleagues has devoted the most effort to this area. Gelso and his colleagues have also focused on developing methods to measure the real relationship. What aspects compose the real relationship? Gelso and his colleagues conclude that there are several fundamental aspects, including genuineness, realism, magnitude, and valence (p. 276).

Gelso, Williams, and Fretz (2014). The Therapeutic Relationship

This book chapter appeared in an edited book by Gelso, Williams, and Fretz on the subject of counseling psychology. They stress the importance of the therapeutic relationship across all modalities of psychotherapy. Also noted is the reciprocal nature of the alliance that includes the interactive contributions of both the patient and therapist. In highlighting their original definition of the therapeutic relationship proposed in 1985 by Gelso and Carter, they note the following important observation:

> Although the relationship has been a key construct in theory and research for many years, little effort has gone into defining just what a therapeutic relationship is and how relationship factors may be differentiated from non-relationship factors. (p. 219)

Gelso et al. (2014) trace the history of conceptualizing the therapeutic relationship from Freud to the present day. Contrary to the idea of the therapeutic relationship being a universal aspect of clinical practice, they find that Freud himself understood the analytic relationship in terms of two aspects—the transference and the positive feelings of the patient to the therapist. The authors remind the reader of the contributions of Ralph Greenson in his landmark formulation that the analytic relationship can be theoretically seen as including three distinct but interactive parts: the working alliance, transference and countertransference, and the real relationship. Gelso et al. (2014) term these as the components of the therapeutic relationship.

Regarding the second aspect of the therapeutic relationship, the transference, Gelso et al. (2014) conclude, "many consider transference to be Freud's most significant discovery. Despite its centrality to psychoanalytic theory, transference (and countertransference) may be considered to be a part of all therapeutic encounters and a component of all therapeutic relationships"

(p. 227). The author's rules of thumb about this critical area are important. That is, transferences are always perceptual errors, can be positive or negative, and are unconscious. The authors define countertransference as "the counselor's transference" (p. 231). As with transferences, they see this counselor's transference as present in all therapeutic encounters regardless of theoretical orientation.

Regarding the last but certainly not least component of the therapeutic relationship, the real relationship, Gelso et al. (2014) highlight the concept of genuineness as central to the real relationship. "We define it as the ability and willingness to be what one truly is in the relationship, to be honest, open, and authentic" (p. 234).

An addition to the chapter is a discussion of "facilitative conditions and therapy relationship" (p. 237). They recognize the three conditions as empathic understanding, unconditional positive regard, and last, genuineness. Gelso et al. (2014) see these conditions are central in developing a working alliance with patients.

SEMINAL PAPERS BY GELSO AND HIS COLLEAGUES

Gelso and Carter (1985). The Relationship in Counseling and Psychotherapy: Components, Consequences, and Theoretical Antecedents

This first article by Gelso and Carter set the bar very high for future work in the area of the therapeutic relationship. That is, the entire issue of this journal was devoted to their 80-page article.

Their article has two parts—the first seeks to define the therapeutic relationship and suggest that it consists of three important components. The article draws from the earlier work of Ralph Greenson (1967). It was Greenson who outlined in detail the three aspects of the therapeutic relationship to include the alliance, transference and counter-transference, and the real relationship. Gelso and Carter (1985) proposed that all therapeutic relationships, regardless of theoretical orientation, include to some degree these three components. Indeed, these three concepts are useful yardsticks to compare psychotherapy approaches. The second part of the article was to apply the tripartite aspects to three major psychotherapies, including psychoanalytic, humanistic, and learning theories. A significant strength of their article is in deriving specific propositions concerning each component.

The authors provide a definition of the therapeutic relationship: "the relationship is the feelings and attitudes that counseling participants have toward one another, and the manner in which these are expressed" (p. 159).

Following that, the authors next review the history and current status of the components of the counseling relationship.

Gelso and Carter (1985) build upon the work of Greenson (1967), who first suggested that the therapeutic relationship consists of three elements: a working alliance, transference-countertransference, and a real relationship. The authors state:

> We would take Greenson's thinking a step further and propose that all thera-
> peutic relationships consist of these three components, although the salience
> and importance of each part during counseling or therapy will vary according
> to the theoretical perspective of the therapist and the particulars of a given
> therapy. (p. 161)

Depending on the theoretical orientation, the alliance is conceptualized differently. For example, an analyst thinks in terms of a "split" in the ego of the patient's and therapist's reasonable parts of themselves. Another view of the alliance is suggested by Bordin's (1975) influential perspective of viewing the working alliance as including a therapist–patient bond and an agreement on the goals and tasks of therapy.

Gelso and Carter (1985) next focus on the topic of transferences, calling these "the unreal relationship in counseling and therapy" (p. 169). The authors view transference and countertransference as "universals"; that is, "transference reactions occur across theoretical persuasions, but that they occur regardless of the duration of treatment" (p. 169). The authors' main conclusion is that transferences are ubiquitous and occur inside and outside of the consulting room (Gelso & Carter, 1985, p. 171).

Gelso and Carter (1985) highlight several important aspects of this process. The first is that transferences involve misperceptions and unconscious processes on the part of patients. To illustrate this, a colleague who is a Catholic priest with an interest in family systems theory remarked that "the clerical collar is the movie screen upon which parishioners show their home movies" (Joe Carolin, personal communication, April 16, 2010). This aspect would of course also apply to ministers, rabbis, and nuns, as well as physicians, nurse practitioners, and therapists. The concept of transference in therapy is emphasized differently depending on the theoretical orientation of the therapist.

The authors suggest the following:

> It is suggested that, although transference does occur in all therapies, how it
> develops and the extent to which it develops as well as its effects depend upon a
> host of factors, most notably the therapist's predilections about its place (or lack
> of it) in counseling. (Gelso & Carter, 1985, p. 173)

Along with transference, there is also the concept of countertransference. Gelso and Carter conclude that countertransferences are the therapist's transferences to their patients. Countertransferences along with their companion concept of transferences are universal in all psychotherapies but conceptualized differently depending on the theory of the provider.

> Thus analytic types will foster by their techniques more transference, whereas humanistic counseling will foster more of a real relationship, and behavior therapy will foster fewer relationship issues in general. (Gelso & Carter, 1985, p. 179)

The real relationship is the last concept discussed. Gelso and Carter (1985) again build on the work of Greenson (1967) who indicated that the real relationship consisted of two important variables—the patient's and therapist's "genuine and realistic perceptions" of each individual (p. 185).

The authors conclude that although the components of the therapeutic alliance can be conceptually separated, the three variables "coexist, side by side" in all psychotherapies (p. 192); however, "each theory has its notion about what is important in the therapeutic relationship" (p. 192).

The second part of Gelso and Carter's (1985) article focuses on how the three components of the therapeutic relationship apply to three major psychotherapy approaches: psychoanalysis, humanism, and learning approaches.

Prior to an extensive discussion of the three major approaches to psychotherapy, the authors seek to compare the psychotherapies along three dimensions of the therapeutic relationship. The first is a centrality dimension, which evaluates a psychotherapy method on whether or not the therapeutic relationship is the central aspect of change (Gelso & Carter, 1985, p. 197). The second dimension is termed the "real-unreal relationship dimension" that focuses on whether the transference relationship or the patient–therapist relationship is most important for a psychotherapy method (Gelso & Carter, 1985, p. 197). The last dimension is a "means-end dimension," which is described as how a particular psychotherapy model views the therapeutic relationship as the mechanism of change or whether there are other variables accounting for behavioral and intra-psychic change (Gelso & Carter, 1985, pp. 197–198).

Comparing three prominent psychotherapy models (psychoanalytic psychotherapy, humanistic approaches, and learning theory) on the three dimensions is an important aspect of the second part of the Gelso and Carter's (1985) article. With psychoanalytic psychotherapy, the therapeutic relationship would rate high on the centrality dimension. The creation of a particular type of therapeutic relationship is one perquisite of this model. Psychoanalytic psychotherapy would also be viewed in the unreal aspect of the real–unreal dimension. This is because a transference is viewed by the authors as the unreal part of the therapeutic relationship. On the last dimension, the means–end variable, the authors place psychoanalytic psychotherapy on the means' side of the continuum because interpretations of transferences are necessary for successful treatment. "The relationship is central in the therapy, but it is the unreal (transferential) aspect on the client's part that is most important" (Gelso & Carter, 1985, p. 203).

In humanistic approaches, as opposed to a focus on transferences, the central attention is on the real relationship. In terms of the three relationship dimensions, the humanistic psychotherapies would be placed on the upper part of the centrality dimension. It is the client–therapist relationship that is central. On the real–unreal dimension, even though transferences are acknowledged, the real relationship is most important. Last, on the question about whether the therapeutic relationship is viewed as a means to an end or an end in itself, it is the creation of a particular type of therapeutic relationship that is critical to a positive outcome in treatment. The person of the therapist is vital to therapy.

Last, with learning theory perspectives, for the centrality aspect the therapeutic relationship is not viewed as a central of change. On the real–unreal dimension, the unreal part of this dimension is deemed not significant. This matches my training in behavior therapy in the mid-1970s, where the particular technique was thought to be the most important aspect in producing change. Last, on the means–end dimension, the means' end of the continuum would be seen as most important.

Gelso and Carter (1994). Components of the Psychotherapy Relationship: Their Interaction and Unfolding during Treatment

About a decade after Gelso and Carter's initial paper, they published another paper on the components of the therapeutic relationship, which concluded the following:

> All therapeutic relationships consist of these three components, although the salience and importance of each part during counseling or therapy will vary according to the theoretical perspective of the therapist and the particulars of a five therapy. (Gelso & Carter, 1994, p. 296)

The components of the therapeutic relationship are not static but interact during treatment in complex ways. Gelso and Carter begin by reviewing their past definition of the therapeutic relationship as well as their conceptualizations of the components (alliance, transference, real relationship). They conclude that the alliance component has received the most theoretical and research attention and that transferences and countertransferences present in all psychotherapies. They also view the last component, the real relationship, with its unique characteristics of genuineness and realism, as receiving the least attention.

The main focus of this article is to evaluate how the three components of the therapeutic relationship interact. As said before, the components are not static, parallel components by dynamic. All three "constantly interact and, to some extent, overlap throughout the course of therapy" (Gelso & Carter, 1994, pp. 298).

The authors make a series of dyadic comparisons between the components. For example, the first was the interaction with transference and the alliance. The authors conclude that transference reactions occur throughout the psychotherapy process so this process would impact the alliance during treatment. In addition, there are aspects of the alliance that are nontransferential. That said both negative and positive transferences strongly impact the alliance and the course of psychotherapy. Conversely, the alliance does influence the transference relationship and both the therapist and patient contribute equally to this process.

The next dyad is the real relationship and the alliance. The authors find that the real relationship has a different impact on the alliance. This is due to the different perceptions that the therapist and patient have of one another. Thus, if the real relationship is mostly positive, then this strengthens the alliance. The reverse is also true.

The last dyad, comparison, is the real relationship and transference. The authors express one conclusion about this. "To the extent that the therapist and client are involved in a real relationship (being genuine and perceiving realistically), they cannot be involved in a transferential one" (Gelso & Carter, 1994, p. 300). In addition, as transference distortions are clarified, accurate perceptions take their place.

The final section of the paper concerns the relationship of the three components alliance or working alliance is thought to be the most basic. That is, the alliance must be viable if psychotherapy can proceed. The authors find that the alliance is not constant but varies throughout psychotherapy. It is also suggested that transferences may be different depending on the length of psychotherapy, brief or longer-term treatment. The final point of the authors is the position of the universality of the real relationship in every psychotherapy method. And, as psychotherapy continues, "the real relationship deepens" (Gelso & Carter, 1994, pp. 304).

Gelso and Bhatia (2012). Crossing Theoretical Lines: The Role and Effects of Transference in Nonanalytic Psychotherapies

This important paper examines the role of the concept of transference in nonanalytic models of psychotherapy. An important point is made in the introduction. That is, in an earlier work, Gelso and Hayes (1998) proposed that "to varying degrees, transference occurs and affects process and outcome in all psychotherapies, regardless of theoretical orientation" (p. 68). Gelso and Hayes also posited that "transference need not be dealt with directly in order for therapy to be effective except in cases in which transference becomes problematic" (p. 89). The above article was undertaken to review the evidence for these propositions.

Gelso and Bhatia's review of the literature suggests that transference is alive and well across the spectrum of psychotherapies. So, transferences occur in both nonanalytic and analytic psychotherapies. However, nonanalytic therapists may not always process transferences in their clinical work. As to the question of how transferences evolve during nonanalytic psychotherapy, Gelso and Bhatia find little empirical work on this issue.

The last question explored by Gelso and Bhatia was the relationship of transference to the course of treatment, patient variables, and outcome in nonanalytic psychotherapies. It does appear that when negative transferences occur during clinical work, therapists will attend to these and seek to resolve the issue with their patients. With the area of the relationship between various patient characteristics, the authors report some findings concerning Bowlby's attachment theory. There is growing evidence "that patient attachment characteristics and attachment-related personality pathologies do relate to the amount and kinds of transferences that emerge with their nonanalytic and analytic therapists alike" (p. 388). The last question related to how transferences influence treatment outcome. It appears that with negative transferences, if the patient has some insight, they have a positive impact on treatment.

Gelso (2014). A Tripartite Model of the Therapeutic Relationship: Theory, Research, and Practice

This was an honorary paper by Gelso for the journal *Psychotherapy Research* highlighting his more than three decades of work on the three components of the therapeutic relationship.

Gelso summarizes his past work as follows:

> In brief, the tripartite model that has evolved over the years posits that all psychotherapy relationships, regardless of the therapist's theoretical orientation,

consists of three interlocking elements: A real relationship, a working alliance, and a transference configuration (consisting of patient transference and therapist countertransference). (p. 117)

Gelso's overall goal with this paper is to "open the package of the relationship and understand its contents" (p. 119). The main thrust of the paper is to detail the three specific components of the tripartite model.

Gelso views the real relationship as the foundation of therapeutic relationships. He also considers the real relationship and the other two sister aspects of the therapeutic relationship as universal in all psychotherapies. Gelso sides with Greenson (1967) in determining the foundation of the real relationship: genuineness and a sense of realism. Gelso also concludes that this component of therapeutic relationship has received the least research focus.

"If the real relationship is the foundation of the overall relationship, the working alliance is what most directly allows the work of psychotherapy to get done" (p. 120). When the therapist and patient unite in their efforts, Gelso believes that the aspects described by Bordin (1979) are present. That is, there is a working bond and agreement on the goals and tasks for successful therapy.

The final component of the therapeutic relationship, transference and countertransference, is termed "conflict and projection" by Gelso (p. 121). The transference component of the tripartite relationship is seen by Gelso as "universal . . . occurring in all psychotherapies and all relationships" (p. 122). For all aspects of the triadic relationship, Gelso (2014) provides definitions for each concept. He also concludes that all three components can be conceptually separate but interact with each other.

Gelso (2014) concludes this seminal paper by addressing a basic question— is there empirical support for the conceptual model of the three triadic relationship? A test of this model by Gelso and one of his colleagues supports this conceptual framework. Of interest, that research reveals four factors—the real relationship, transference, countertransference, and the alliance. So, he indicates a *quadripartite* model may be more appropriate than the well-known term of a triadic model of the therapeutic relationship.

RESEARCH ON COMPONENTS OF THE THERAPEUTIC RELATIONSHIP

Gelso and Gelso and his colleagues have made significant contributions to the research on the components of the therapeutic relationship as well as theory, especially in the areas of transference, countertransference, and the real relationship.

In research on transferences, Gelso, Hill, and Kivlighan (1991) examined the interaction of transference, insight, and therapist intentions during psychotherapy. They determined that this interaction impacted session quality when insight and transferences were added together.

Gelso, Kivlighan, Wine, Jones, and Friedman (1997) studied how transference and insight developed in time-limited psychotherapy. An interaction between transference and insight contributed to both therapist and patient outcomes. That is, the outcome in brief therapy was associated with the therapist's assessment of the degree of transference and insight occurring early in the treatment process. Gelso, Hill, Mohr, Rochlen, and Zack (1999) used a qualitative research model to study transference in therapist perceptions in long-term psychotherapy. The basis for this study was phone interviews with 11 psychodynamically oriented psychotherapists. Transference developed in a complex manner over the course of therapy with no consistent pattern.

With the topic of countertransferences, Wagoner, Gelso, Hayes, and Diemer (1991) examined therapists rated as *excellent* and how they differed from other therapists in managing countertransferences. Those therapists categorized as *excellent* when compared to other therapists had more insight, more capacity for empathy, more understanding of patient emotions, displayed less anxiety, and were better able to conceptualize the patient's history and current presentation. Gelso, Fassinger, Gomez, and Latts (1995) evaluated countertransference reactivity to lesbian patients. In this study, countertransference reaction with therapists of both genders was studied in reference to reactions to an actor's sexual orientation (lesbian or heterosexual). Contrary to predictions, no support was found for therapists' ability to manage countertransference reactions with the two sexual orientations. Latts and Gelso (1995) studied the countertransference behaviors of therapists working with sexual assault survivors. This study used a two-step model of countertransference management. The two-step model teaches an awareness of the therapist's countertransference behaviors and then suggests a neutral position to allow interpretation of these behaviors. The study failed to replicate a past study in that therapists rated highly on emotional awareness did not demonstrate less countertransference behavior. Support was found when a theoretical perspective was combined with increased levels of clinical awareness.

Gelso and Hayes (2001) discussed the issue of countertransference management by evaluating the five factors seen as necessary in the management of this problem. The factors necessary in managing countertransference received some preliminary support. These factors are self-insight, self-integration, management of anxiety, empathy, and ability to conceptualize clinical problems.

Drawing on the transtheoretical work of Bordin, therapist attachment styles, and the working alliance, Ligiero and Gelso (2002) found that countertransference behaviors are related to aspects of the working alliance. Managing countertransference behaviors and the outcome of therapy were evaluated by Gelso, Latts, Gomez, and Fassinger (2002). Preliminary support was provided for the importance of managing countertransference.

An overall review of the management of countertransference was completed by Gelso and Hayes (2002) for an edited work by Norcross titled *Psychotherapy Relationships That Work.* A review of the meta-analyses on the empirical work on the management of countertransference was completed by Hayes, Gelso, and Hummel (2011). The results of this meta-analysis found some association of countertransference with reduced psychotherapy outcomes. Countertransference management appears important in reducing the reactions to countertransference issues. If unmanaged, countertransference can interfere with treatment. Last, Fuertes, Gelso, Owen, and Cheng (2013) examine the use of the Inventory of Countertransference Behavior (ICB) for observers. The ICB was originally published in 2000.

It is with the real relationship aspect of the therapeutic relationship that Gelso and his colleagues have made their greatest contribution to the research literature. For example, Gelso, Kelly, Marmarosh, Holmes, Costa, and Hancock (2005) provided an important contribution by developing and validating the Real Relationship Inventory-Therapist form (RRI-T). This 24-item inventory was found to have adequate reliability and validity. The RRI-T provides an important measure of the real relationship aspects of the therapeutic relationship.

Fuertes, Mislowack, Brown, Gur-Arsie, Wilkinson, and Gelso (2007) studied both patient and therapist ratings of the real relationship in the context of their working alliance ratings. There was a positive association of the ratings of the real relationship, working alliance, and the patient's progress in treatment. Another study of the real relationship in psychotherapy evaluated this relationship to adult attachment, working alliance, transference, and symptoms from both the patient and the therapist (Marmarosh et al., 2009). This study evaluated the real relationship in the early stages of psychotherapy. "The therapist rating of the real relationship was the only significant predictor of post treatment symptoms" (p. 347).

Gelso (2009) provided a review of both empirical and theoretical aspects of the real relationship in this theoretical review. He conceptualizes the real relationship as consisting of two fundamental aspects—realism and genuineness. On the basis of past work, Gelso views the real relationship as distinct from the alliance and the transference. Gelso (2009) outlines two measures of the real relationship—the Real Relationship Inventory that has both therapist and patient versions. As a follow-up to Gelso's (2009) article, Kelly, Gelso, Fuertes, Marmarosh, and Lanier (2010) provide a report of the psychometric development of the patient version of the Real Relationship Inventory. The association of the real relationship and working alliance in psychotherapy is provided by Lo Coco, Gullo, Prestano, and Gelso (2011). This was the first study of the real relationship outside the United States; it was completed at the University of Palermo in Sicily. An interesting finding of this study concerned the working alliance, which found no association to treatment outcome.

In the last study in this series of research on the real relationship, Moore and Gelso (2011) studied a sample of 143 undergraduates and report on their experiences in psychotherapy and interrelations of attachment and memories of their therapists. As predicted, the rating of the real relationship was associated with patient's positive attachment to their therapist. Gullo, Lo Coco, and Gelso (2012) studied early and late predictors of outcome during brief psychotherapy. Compared to patients who terminate psychotherapy, the real relationship is more significant for patients who continue in psychotherapy. The real relationship is an important aspect of positive treatment outcome early in the treatment process. Gelso et al. (2012) address the association of the real relationship of both patients and therapists and outcome in brief psychotherapy. The study focused on 42 patient–therapist dyads. An overall finding was that the real relationship developing between patient and therapist is a positive factor in outcome. Patients continuing in psychotherapy rate their real relationship as strong. Over time the therapist evaluations of the real relationship matched the patient ratings, and this is related to positive outcome.

Fuertes, Gelso, Owen, and Cheng (2013) utilized six patient–therapist dyads to study how the real relationship develops during psychotherapy with the dimensions of working alliance, patient's transference, and therapist's countertransference. In terms of the research questions, the real relationship development seems to depend on which person is doing the ratings and on treatment outcome. The real relationship progresses when the working alliance is related to outcome. With the variables of transference and countertransference, transference is reduced in successful psychotherapy but increases with problematic treatment. Negative countertransferences also increase with less successful psychotherapy cases.

A fundamental question examined by Markin, Kivlighan, Gelso, Hummel, and Spiegel (2014) is whether there is an association between ratings on the real relationship and the session quality for both therapists and patients. Using the Actor Partner Interdependence Model (APIM), the real relationship becomes a predictor of positive outcome in psychotherapy. An important clinical suggestion is that therapists must work to establish a strong real relationship from the onset of psychotherapy.

In a study reviewed by Kivlighan, Gelso, Ain, Hummel, and Markin (2015), there was a reanalysis of the earlier study by Gelso et al. (2012). It was a replication study that concluded that differences between therapists explain real relationship variables and positive outcome in psychotherapy. Last, Kivlighan, Hill, Gelso, and Baumann (2015) use the Actor Partner Interdependence Model (APIM) to evaluate patient and therapist perceptions of the alliance and real relationship and quality of therapy sessions. The results suggest a complex interaction: "therapist and client's ratings of session quality are related to a complex interplay of relationship variables, time, and patient improvement" (p. 11). The results also suggest the importance of ongoing monitoring of the real relationship and attention to the working alliance in the early stages of psychotherapy.

Gelso and his colleagues have made lasting contributions by introducing the triadic model of the therapeutic relationship to a new generation of psychotherapy clinicians and researchers. In addition, they operationally defined the three components of the triadic model and provided significant bodies of research on two of the components of the therapeutic relationship—transference and countertransference—and the real relationship. Part of their research effort was to develop and psychometrically test instruments to measure various components of the therapeutic relationship.

In the next chapter, I will return to a review of William Meissner's conceptualization of the nature of the therapeutic relationship useful in comparing psychotherapy methods.

Chapter Three

The Contributions of
W. W. Meissner, SJ, MD

William W. Meissner, SJ, MD (1931–2010), was a remarkable individual who wore two hats; he was a Jesuit priest and a psychoanalyst. According to memorial tributes by Ana-Maria Rizzuto, MD, William Massicotte, PhD, and Harold Bursztan, MD, he authored more than 285 publications, including 27 books. His diverse work in many areas included psychoanalysis, psychoanalytic theory, psychoanalysis and religion, and the therapeutic relationship. Dr. Meissner was a training and supervising analyst at Boston Psychoanalytic Institute, and University Professor of Psychoanalysis at Boston College. It was his book, *The Therapeutic Alliance*, that attracted my attention about the same time that I was researching Dr. Bowen's papers in the History of Medicine Division of the National Library of Medicine. Dr. Meissner's book provided a framework for conceptualizing the nature of the therapeutic relationship and a useful template to compare psychotherapy methods. His work presents details concerning the nuances of this basic concept and remains a major contribution to psychoanalytic psychotherapy and psychotherapy in general.

I sent the first paper that I wrote on Bowen's Family Study Project to Dr. Meissner. I was not seeking comments per se, although his thoughts would have been most welcomed, but I told him that his book provided a framework for my work on how family psychotherapy emerged during Bowen's Family Study Project. To my surprise, he reviewed the paper, later published in *Family Systems*, and wrote me a long email. He recalled fondly his days with Dr. Bowen working on multigenerational family histories during his time at Georgetown University. Dr. Meissner also provided some useful thinking about the process of family psychotherapy and how a therapeutic relationship with this orientation differs from a conventional approach.

I would like to think that Dr. Meissner's first paper, "Thinking about the Family-Psychiatric Aspects," published in *Family Process* in 1964, was related to his work with Murray Bowen. Dr. Meissner's early paper about families reflected a style repeated in his many future publications—comprehensive and with detailed documentation. For example, this 13-page paper on the family had 135 references. His survey and evaluation of the theory and practice about family therapy at that time reflected the *Psychological Bulletin* articles of today.

This chapter is a small tribute highlighting Dr. Meissner's papers in the area of the therapeutic relationship. Meissner published one book in this area titled *The Therapeutic Alliance* in 1996. This book will not be reviewed. Following the article reviews, commentaries are provided highlighting the relevance to family systems theory.

All areas of mental health, including clinical social work, psychiatry, clinical psychology, counseling, and nursing, owe a great debt to the work of Dr. Meissner in this basic and critical area. Many wrote about the therapeutic relationship, but it was Dr. Meissner who provided a way to conceptualize this fundamental subject. The therapeutic relationship remains the bedrock of clinical practice for all models of psychotherapy, psychology, nursing, and counseling.

REVIEW OF MEISSNER'S ARTICLES ON THE THERAPEUTIC RELATIONSHIP

The Concept of the Therapeutic Alliance (1992)

This was the initial paper written by Dr. Meissner on the therapeutic alliance. He begins by tracing the history of the concept of the therapeutic alliance beginning with Freud, later with Zetzel in 1956, and continuing with Greenson in 1965.

He begins the article by indicating apparent misperceptions over the term *therapeutic alliance*. For example, historically some analysts have equated the term only with the concept of transference (Meissner, 1992). He next continues with a brief historical review. Meissner (1992) notes that Freud (1912) came close to describing the alliance when he spoke of an aspect of the transference. The next milestone in the historical chronology was Sterba's work in 1934 in which he stressed the difference between the transference and the alliance. Following Sterba (1934), Zetzel (1956) broadened the concept of the transference (Meissner, 1992). It was Greenson (1965) who first used the term *working alliance* (Meissner, 1992). Greenson conceptualized the working alliance in terms of the idea of rationality between the egos of the analyst and the patient (Meissner, 1992).

It was these early formulations according to Meissner (1992) that contributed some degree of confusion to conceptualizing the concept of the therapeutic alliance. This was due to a lack of clarity between the concepts of the alliance, transference, countertransference, and the real relationship (Meissner, 1992). Meissner's basic conclusion was that the three concepts interact continually but can be conceptually separated. Including the alliance, transference and countertransference, and the real relationship in the therapeutic relationship and distinguishing these is the goal of his first paper.

The next part of Meissner's article highlights some of the differences between the alliance, transference, and the real relationship in various clinical situations. For example, the alliance comes into play from the onset of the therapeutic relationship while the transference may not.

Various aspects of reality are important in the therapeutic relationship. For example, there are the realities of the office of the therapist and of course the personal characteristics of the therapist. The alliance reflects important interactions between the therapist and the patient necessary for effective clinical work.

But how can the alliance be operationalized? In one way the alliance may include aspects of the therapeutic relationship besides the concepts of transference and countertransference. Meissner (1992) finishes this initial article by discussing important central aspects of the alliance. He also views empathy as essential in therapeutic encounters. The therapeutic framework, including the required elements for clinical engagement, is discussed next. These elements are responsibility, authority, freedom, trust, autonomy, initiative, and, interestingly, ethics. He views ethics as being involved in every action of the therapeutic alliance, such that departures from the alliance place the alliance in jeopardy.

In conclusion, Meissner (1992) seeks to demonstrate the importance of the therapeutic alliance and its connection to other important aspects of the therapeutic relationship, including transference/countertransference and the real relationship. Meissner (1992) also believes that the alliance may be as important to a positive outcome as transference management and interpretation.

Empathy in the Therapeutic Alliance (1996b)

In this article Meissner focused on what he thought was the most important aspect of the therapeutic relationship—empathy. At the onset, he restates his basic assumption that that the therapeutic relationship in psychoanalytic psychotherapy contains three conceptually distinct but interrelated concepts, which include the alliance, the transference, and the real relationship.

Meissner (1996b) summarizes his central idea that the alliance has many aspects not related to transferences and countertransferences. He argues that empathy is the essential aspect of the therapeutic relationship.

Meissner (1996b) makes the point that the variable of empathy may be like a normally distributed variable; that is, there are degrees of empathy in therapists. Some have a high degree while others have a moderate degree. In addition, Meissner (1996a) also views empathy as a two-way street since both the therapist and the patient must have some degree of empathy for a successful therapeutic relationship to occur. Thus, a solid therapeutic alliance reflects solid empathic responses on the part of both the therapist and the patient.

Neutrality, Abstinence, and the Therapeutic Alliance (1998)

This article highlights two other variables, in addition to empathy, that Meissner considers critical in the practice of psychoanalysis. These are neutrality and abstinence. Empathy, neutrality, and abstinence make an interesting triad.

Meissner begins the article by stating that neutrality has long been held as an indispensable aspect of analytic practice. Freud's use of the term came to mean how the therapist effectively managed countertransferences.

By way of definition, Meissner finds that neutrality and abstinence are different processes and should be defined differently. Neutrality reflects a perspective about attitudes and judgments of the therapist, whereas abstinence refers to reactions to the behavior of the patient.

Meissner states that neutrality can have negative connotations. For example, neutrality can suggest indifference or a lack of concern. It would appear that many therapists know what neutrality is in a practical sense but may find it hard to define this concept. The word *abstinence* has the same problem. Meissner argues that neutrality should be viewed from the perspective of the alliance. Neutrality can imply detachment. This difficulty has arisen from the time of Freud, who used the metaphor of a mirror that implied noninvolvement.

An important aspect of neutrality is that there are times that the therapist cannot and should not be neutral. Meissner gives two clinical examples. The first is a patient presenting with a severe cut from broken glass. In this instance, the therapist suggested that she seek immediate medical care. In another example of a suicidal patient, the therapist was not indifferent to this presentation and suggested hospitalization.

In summary, Meissner believes that neutrality is not synonymous with several of the negative images associated with the concept, such as indifference. He sees neutrality and abstinence as different but related terms. Neutrality from an analytic perspective entails a therapeutic view regardless of what arises in the clinical session. Abstinence is a middle of the road plan, that is, whether to give in or unnecessarily frustrate the patient. Meissner thinks that both processes are important components of psychoanalytic treatment. In addition, they are important aspects of the therapeutic alliance. While both are usually considered actions by the therapist, they apply equally to both therapist and patient.

Notes on the Therapeutic Role of the Alliance (1999)

In this article, Meissner notes that the idea of the *therapeutic alliance* has existed since Freud. He provides significant details about the history of the principals who have contributed to specifying the concept of the therapeutic alliance as well as the other aspects, including the transference-countertransference and the real relationship. As Meissner commented, these components are constantly present and interactive elements of the therapeutic relationship, but for heuristic purposes they require separate description (p. 1).

This particular paper is more about the history and the development of the elements of the therapeutic relationship than his book is. Another topic not mentioned in his past papers is the positive association between therapeutic alliances and outcomes. Likewise, a problematic alliance can foster premature terminations in psychotherapy. Meissner cites a litany of areas beyond individual psychotherapy from a psychoanalytic perspective where the importance of the therapeutic relationship has been noted. These include family therapy, clinical work with children and adolescents, group psychotherapy, general medical practice, psychiatry emergency room visits, posttraumatic stress disorders, eating disorders, multiple personalities, schizophrenia, and even medication management. Meissner views the alliance as an interactive process of personalities between the therapist and the patient.

The Many Faces of the Analytic Interaction (2000)

This is the first article Meissner completed for a nonpsychiatric journal, *Psychoanalytic Psychology*. He again referred to his familiar theme, that is, "the triune construction of the analytic relation" (p. 513). He again argues the following:

> The therapeutic relation is composed of three distinct components: transference, real relation, and alliance—all of which are interactive and involve participative action on the part of both participants, analyst and analysand. (p. 513)

One reason to work toward conceptually keeping the three aspects of the therapeutic relationship separate is that "the prevailing tendency is to pay almost exclusive attention to the transference (and countertransference) interaction and to ignore or minimize other components" (p. 514). Meissner highlights the importance of nontransferential aspects of the therapeutic relationship.

There are some new things in this article other than Meissner's main theme of the conceptual effort to keep the three concepts of the therapeutic relationship separate. He also notes historical confusion with the alliance and real relationship. For example, the real relationship is termed the *therapeutic alliance* by Zetzel, and the *working alliance* by Greenson. This kind of confusing terminology reinforces Meissner's emphasis to keep the three elements of the therapeutic relationship separate.

There are some other interesting aspects to this article. First is Meissner's discussion of just what is meant by the term *real relationship*. Meissner notes that some controversy exists about the exact meaning of *real*. Some of the literature refers to the real relationship in terms of personality characteristics of the therapist and the patient. Meissner, however, brings up an interesting additional aspect of the real relationship. He writes:

> In my view, a firm distinction exists between psychic reality and the actual reality of the real persons involved in the analytic transaction, and I would contend further that the basic prerequisite for cure in analysis lies in alliance rather than in the real relationship. Correspondingly, it is not the real person who engages in the alliance, but the analytic in his role as therapeutic agent. (p. 520)

Second, Meissner comments concerning the parental model. He notes:

> The therapist does not need to be, and cannot be, a better parent. The therapist can be someone the patient might have *wished* to have as his or her parent, but the therapist cannot *be* that parent. We can only be the therapist. The unsafe therapist is the therapist who wants to be anything other than a therapist. (p. 526)

In summary, Meissner notes that the therapeutic relationship has three aspects that are distinct but continually interact. In addition, the therapist and the patient both contribute to the therapeutic relationship. The alliance is also seen as the primary vehicle for effective treatment. The concept of transference/countertransference and real relationship can impact the alliance and at times can lead to misalliances.

The Therapeutic Alliance—A Proteus in Disguise (2006a)

This is an article written as part of a special section of *Psychotherapy: Theory, Research, Practice, Training* of six other papers on the working alliance (see Castonguay, Constantino, & Holtforth, 2006; Crits-Christoph, Gibbons, &

Hearon, 2006; Hatcher & Barends, 2006; Horvath, 2006; Safran & Muran, 2006; Samstag, 2006).

In his introductory comments, Meissner (2006) notes:

> I would maintain that it is ubiquitous and universal, as well as essential, perspective in all psychoanalytic and other therapeutic endeavors. Although my own orientation is psychoanalytic, I view the alliance as an operative factor in all therapies. (p. 264)

Meissner's article provides an overview of his thinking about the triadic nature of the therapeutic relationship for a new audience who may not have known about his past writings on the subject. He also believes that the alliance should not be viewed in isolation but rather as one aspect of the therapeutic relationship. In a concise definition, he defined the alliance as "those factors and dimensions of the analytic relation that constitute the therapeutic pact and determine the context within which effective therapeutic interventions, interactions, and interpretive communication can take place" (p. 265). He viewed transference and countertransference as providing "the materials on which the psychoanalytic process works" (p. 265). Last, the real relationship reflects "their existence and status as real persons functioning in the real world" (p. 265). Meissner (2006) concludes that it is important to acknowledge the importance alliance factors play in all types of clinical practice.

Finding and Refining the Therapeutic Alliance: On Thinking and Thirds (2006b)

In the first section of this article, Meissner returns to his familiar concern with the tripartite nature of the analytic relationship. The details of this have been reviewed in his past articles.

What is new in this article are his comments on mentalization and the concept of the analytic third. Mentalization is a concept that is familiar to some clinicians today. It reflects a joint position of the therapist and the patient to understand human behavior in terms of mental states in the context of attachment relationships. Meissner concludes that the therapist's mentalizing position identifies his/her position in the alliance. In addition, mentalizing involves empathy on the part of the therapist that for Meissner is a critical component of the alliance.

Last, Meissner discusses the analytic third. The analytic third is a concept elaborated by some authors where the subjective interaction between the analyst and the patient becomes a third subject in the room. Meissner finds this concept problematic. The therapist and the patient are "real subjects and between them is a real relation. But a relation is not a separate thing with existence in its own right" (p. 673).

Therapeutic Alliance: Themes and Variations (2007)

This article is the last completed by Meissner on the subject of the therapeutic relationship and its components. Even though the concept of the alliance originated within psychoanalytic psychotherapy, Meissner concludes that the alliance operates within all therapeutic contexts.

Meissner next considers the relationship between the alliance and the outcome in psychotherapy. Research studies find that "the quality of the alliance between therapist and patient is a critical variable in predicting outcome" (p. 236). Meissner next reviews the varieties of the alliance that extend beyond individual psychoanalytic psychotherapy. For example, he considers child analysis, hospital work, clinical work with a variety of diagnoses, family therapy, general medical practice, and psychiatric emergencies as forms of behavior therapy. Meissner also reviews other contexts such as supervision, forensic psychiatry, and inpatient and outpatient medical care. In all of these diverse settings, Meissner notes the importance of the therapeutic alliance as essential to the success of any of these efforts.

SUMMARY

In the ending of Gelso and Samstag's (2008) book chapter on the tripartite model of the therapeutic relationship, they conclude with observations about some challenges for research in this area. There is a natural conflict between theory building and research. The enduring contributions of Meissner and Gelso and his colleagues reflect this. Meissner's work reflected an interest in the theory of the components of the therapeutic relationship, whereas Gelso and his colleagues have made significant strides in research on these aspects.

In the next chapters, I will begin my analysis of the relationship between the therapeutic relationship and the family systems therapy as developed by Murray Bowen, by providing a synopsis of his original papers and the emergence of family psychotherapy.

Part Three

Chapter Four

Reviews of Historical Papers in Family Psychotherapy[1]

> According to my thinking, there is nothing in schizophrenia that is not also present in all of us. Schizophrenia is made of the essence of human experience, many times distilled. With our incapacity to look at ourselves, we have much to learn about ourselves from studying the least mature of us. (Bowen, 2013, p. 121)

Bowen's NIMH Family Study Project conducted from 1954 to 1959 was a historic undertaking. While there were many significant findings, the event attracting the most attention from the numerous project visitors was the daily staff–patient groups, later called family psychotherapy. However, the role of the family psychotherapist was a major departure from the one in traditional individual psychoanalytic psychotherapy. It is the purpose of this article to review chronologically several important unpublished and published papers from the Family Study Project that highlight the creation and early development of the practice of family psychotherapy.

Students of Bowen family systems theory are familiar with summaries of Bowen's Family Study Project at NIMH. They are detailed in several chapters of *Family Therapy in Clinical Practice* as well as in other publications and videos. However, many of the original project papers are not as well known. Bowen's published papers on the NIMH project are the second act of a two-act play; the original papers are act 1.

The NIMH Family Study Project was really two studies in one: the first year and the last three years. During the first year, three mother–daughter pairs were admitted to an inpatient unit for evaluation and study. The dyads were selected based on the intensity of dyadic symbiosis rather than severity of the child's symptoms. Based on observations and clinical experiences with these dyads, it was found that symptoms in patients were part of a process

43

involving the entire family. Thus, during the last three years of the project, the attention was on family units, and the concept of the family as an emotional unit was developed and clarified. Intertwined with this concept, family psychotherapy was initiated and refined as one method of treating family units. This article explains how family psychotherapy evolved during Bowen's research project and summarizes important elements of clinical practice during the last three years of the Family Study Project. Seven individual papers will be reviewed chronologically with attention to the background and analysis of each paper and what it illustrates about the theory and practice of family psychotherapy during the Family Study Project.

INFLUENCE OF THE EARLY MOTHER–CHILD RELATIONSHIP IN THE DEVELOPMENT OF SCHIZOPHRENIA, DECEMBER 1955

Background

This project description sheet documents the first mention of the concept of the family as an emotional unit. The paper represents a significant shift in the direction of the project research from conceptualizing symptoms in the patient to a family process that gets focused in one person (Bowen, 1955a). This project description sheet records this change in direction from mother–daughter dyads to a family project.

> Proposed Course of the Project: A shift from seeing schizophrenia as a process between mother and patient or as an illness within the patient influenced by the mother to an orientation of seeing schizophrenia as the manifestation of a distraught family that becomes focused in one individual. The course will be to see the project as a "family project" rather than a "mother-patient" project. (Bowen, 2013, p. 25)

Analysis

This brief paper was written 14 months after the project started. A major finding was "a rapidly growing awareness of the importance of father or other family figures important to the mother" (Bowen, 2013, p. 25). In the last section on the proposed course of the project, it was concluded that fathers or other family figures would be included. At the end of 1955, the first family was admitted. The direction of the project was changed to a family project rather than a mother–patient project. A final important comment was made by Bowen (2013) by noting that the clinical efforts were "an attempt to work out techniques to be therapeutically helpful to the family as a unit rather than isolating the various family members for individual help through psychotherapy" (Bowen, 2013, p. 26).

THE TREATMENT OF SCHIZOPHRENIA USING MODIFICATION OF PSYCHOANALYTIC TECHNIQUES AND EXTENSION OF PSYCHOANALYTIC THEORY, JULY 1956

Background

In this seminal 14-page paper, Bowen (Bowen, 1956c) discusses the character and intensity of the transference phenomenon in psychotic patients. The paper focuses on a particular issue: how the development of transferences in psychotic patients differs from transferences in neurotic patients. This is the only paper that contains an extensive discussion of the transference–countertransference phenomenon with project families. Last, a review of the last part of the title is instructive, "modifications of psychoanalytic techniques and extension of psychoanalytic theory" (Bowen, 2013, p. 45). The title reflects an extension of theory.

> The specific approach to this project would go in the direction of attempting to treat schizophrenia by techniques which attempt to keep the transference on the level of intensity of neurotic transference. A general theme comes into focus. One point would be that the therapist might develop techniques in which he did not lend himself to the patient's bid that he does a certain amount of "replacing the parent." Experience would indicate that the patients do in fact need such a figure. If this be so, then who should this figure be? To what extend is it not so? (p. 47)

Analysis

This paper has several important aspects. First, it is the only paper with several hand-drawn illustrations. Second, there is a detailed discussion of transference difficulties with psychotic patients. Specifically, Bowen (1956c) notes that transferences are more intense and primitive with psychotic patients. One question became how to reduce the intensity and primitive nature of the transferences to the level of neurotic patients.

Third is the issue of working to psychologically replace parents that often occurred in analysis. "It might be said that it is a goal that the therapist replace the parent in psychological importance and that a major therapeutic principle is the analysis of this relationship" (Bowen, 2013, p. 46). This quote described one aspect of a traditional therapeutic relationship in psychoanalytic psychotherapy. However, a goal of family psychotherapy was to avoid psychologically replacing a parent or parents. For this time period, this was a dramatic shift from traditional practice.

Bowen next outlines a conceptual scheme where the schizophrenic "patient is shown in two contrasting dichotomies" (Bowen, 2013, pp. 47–48). He illustrates this by a circle divided in two halves—one for a mature side and the other for an immature side. The model at that time was to control responses to the patient's immaturity and have the patient communicate "as a mature person speaking about immaturity rather than a person relating with his immaturity" (Bowen, 2013, p. 48). However, this is not always easy or straightforward. "In our experience, the greatest problem is unwitting response to the immature side in spite of all effort to control this" (Bowen, 2013, p. 49).

Regarding specific methods, "the therapists would find it easier not to become incorporated into the symbiosis and that the ward staff stay neutral and supporting and above all stay out of the symbiotic conflict" (Bowen, 2013, p. 49). Working to avoid the symbiotic conflict was the opposite of traditional analytic practice.

The therapeutic philosophy was to do the following:

> Stay out of immature attachments. This is more precisely said to be helpful while staying detached from the other person's immaturities. It is in helping with a problem without becoming responsible for the problem. Our technical problem therefore is very small in being helpful and very great in preventing over helpfulness. (Bowen, 2013, p. 54)

A PSYCHOLOGICAL FORMULATION OF SCHIZOPHRENIA, AUGUST 1956

Background

This paper was originally written in August 1956. It was published in *Family Systems* in 1995, with an introduction by Catherine Rakow. This is a comprehensive history of Bowen's thinking in the area of schizophrenia before and during the NIMH research. This paper highlights Bowen's attention to theoretical formulations about schizophrenia and how theory and extensions in theory lead to changes in clinical practices.

> The present formulation regards schizophrenia in the patient as part of a problem that involves the entire family. The family is seen as a psychological unit and the individual family member as part of the larger family unit. The

therapeutic effort is directed to the family as a unit rather than to any individual in the unit. (Bowen, 1995, p. 19)

Analysis

Whereas this is an excellent historical paper on Bowen's evolution of theory, this paper is reviewed here because of the contributions it makes in understanding the theory and practice of family psychotherapy during the Family Study Project.

Bowen related that experiences at the Menninger Clinic in the treatment of inpatient and outpatient schizophrenic patients led to interpretations about this clinical problem. At that time it was widely accepted that poor mothering played a part in the development of schizophrenic symptoms. Illustrating how theory influenced practice, the treatment went in the direction "to neutralize the effects of the inadequate mothering" (Bowen, 2013, p. 26).

> The therapist was very quickly in the role of replacement parent. The relationship seemed best described by the term "symbiotic." Observations of the patients in these relationships showed no elements to support the unconscious rejection theory. It seemed more appropriate to think of the relationship as a primary positive over-attachment between mother and patient. (Bowen, 2013, p. 27)

Bowen provided rich details about the origins, operations, and complexity of symbiosis in families. He also concluded "that there is a wide range of persisting symbiotic unions extending from the very mild to the very intense attachments" (Bowen, 1995, p. 32). In other words, symbiosis exists on a continuum. Last, in deference to the concept of the family as an emotional unit, he noted, "the father plays a reciprocating role to the mother-child symbiotic union" (Bowen, 1995, p. 32).

> At the beginning of the research project, the mother was still seen as all-important in the relationship with the patient but she was no longer seen as the harmful one who had hurt the patient. Instead, she and the patient were seen as two people who had done the best they could with a difficult situation. (p. 33)

The therapy process was described as analysis of family relationships rather than the analysis of the patient–therapist transference relationship. It was an important finding that it was unnecessary to analyze transferences in order to be helpful to family members.

The article closes by restating the importance of the perspective of the family as a single unit. The symptoms in the patient are understood as involving the entire family. The patient–staff meetings, or family unit therapy as it was known early on, enabled Bowen "to be in a reasonably objective psychotherapeutic relationship to schizophrenia" (Bowen, 1995, p. 42).

THE DEVELOPMENT OF TECHNIQUES
OF DEALING WITH FIVE FAMILY UNITS
AND SOME PATTERNS OBSERVED IN THE
TRANSACTION OF THESE FAMILIES, 1957

Background

This paper is really part of a trilogy. That is, it is a first draft of a paper that was revised and later published with a different title. This last paper was presented on March 8, 1957, at a meeting of the American Orthopsychiatry Association in Chicago, Illinois.

> Our approach is to return to the patient the other members of the family and to allow the real family to be the patient's material for this reconstitution and development of intense relationship. (Bowen, Dysinger, Brodey, & Basamania, 1957a, p. 5)

Analysis

This draft paper contains an important discussion of the issue of therapeutic difficulties and their possible resolution. A dilemma occurs when the therapist is placed or assumes the role of parent. In the classical sense, this role is a necessary part of the therapy process. However, from this position much objectivity is lost, and the therapeutic relationship can become very intense. But such a role is necessary in establishing a therapeutic relationship. If this role is abandoned, then what will take its place? How can therapy then proceed? Bowen and his colleagues worked to "allow the real family to be the patient's material for this reconstitution and development of intense relationship" (Bowen et al., 1957, p. 5). This presents an opportunity for the therapist to be less involved and better able to interpret family processes. A move from perceiving the emotional unit as the family instead of the individual aids in the process of not adopting parental functions with patients.

THE FAMILY AS THE UNIT OF STUDY
AND TREATMENT WORKSHOP, 1959

Background

At the end of the Family Study Project in 1959, Bowen and his colleagues presented an all-day workshop titled The Family as the Unit of Study and Treatment Workshop. There were four presentations, one by each of the investigators. All the papers were later published in 1961 in the *American Journal of Orthopsychiatry.* Dr. Bowen wrote the lead paper.

> The therapeutic effort is to analyze existing interfamily relationships *in situ*, rather than to analyze the transference relationship between patient and analyst. When the therapy is successful in relating to the family unit and in avoiding individual relationships, the family unit develops a dependence on the therapist similar to neurotic transference, which is unlike the intense primitive attachment of psychotic patients to the therapist. (Bowen, 2013, p. 112)

Analysis

Bowen's paper on *Family Psychotherapy* appears as chapter 5 in *Family Therapy in Clinical Practice* but includes an introduction that does not appear in his book. The introduction is an excellent summary of the project and provides important details about sample size, that is, the number of families involved in the research.

Bowen begins his paper with the observation that family psychotherapy in the project was derived from the concept of "the family as the unit of illness" (Bowen, 2013, p. 105). He also outlines an important developmental perspective on symbiotic attachments with mothers and their schizophrenic children.

> The basic character problem, on which psychotic symptoms were superimposed, was considered to be an unresolved symbiotic attachment to the mother. The symbiotic attachment was regarded as an arrest in the normal psychological growth process between mother and child, which was initiated by the infant's response to the emotional immaturity of the mother, which neither wanted and against which both have struggled unsuccessfully over the years. (Bowen, 2013, p. 105)

There were challenges in the application of the concept of the family as an emotional unit; if one's attention is on the family unit, then it is critical to relate to the family unit and not become overinvolved with individual family members. This difficulty was an ongoing problem. "My efforts have gone toward recognizing individual involvements when they occur, and toward finding more efficient ways to regain and to maintain emotional detachment" (Bowen, 2013, p. 116).

The roles of the family psychotherapist were also clearly defined. First, the therapist needs to take a "position of unbiased detachment from which position he is able to analyze intrafamily forces" (Bowen, 2013, p. 112). The family psychotherapist must also defer in the analysis of the transference relationship between patient and therapist. Bowen did not avoid the topic of transference and countertransference but concluded that the intensity of transferences could be reduced but not eliminated by treating the family unit.

Bowen's last observation about the role of the family psychotherapist was in searching for a family leader. Finding a leader was often a challenge because the family presented as a helpless unit. However, nurturing the position of a family leader was important. Part of the family leader's job description entailed being the family spokesperson but not an assistant therapist.

THE EMOTIONAL LIFE OF THE FAMILY: INFERENCES FOR SOCIAL CASEWORK

Background

This paper by Basamania (Bowen, 2013) is the last in the series of presentations in The Family as the Unit of Study and Treatment Workshop in 1959. Since she was the only clinical social worker on the project, Basamania's interest was from a social casework perspective.

> The research project offered an apt framework for the study of the emotional life of the family unit and for the development of an approach to the unit. The theoretical orientation regarded the schizophrenic problem as part of the process that involved the entire family. Systematic observations of family units were consistent with this hypothesis, and treatment, based upon these observations, was adapted to the family unit. (Bowen, 2013, p. 138)

Analysis

Early in her article, Basamania shows appreciation for the concept of the family as an emotional unit, noting that an individual perspective masked important observations. In another important conclusion, Basamania (2013) finds that the concept of the family as an emotional unit significantly alters the traditional therapist–patient relationship.

More specifically, she finds that effective therapy is not possible if the therapist has relationships with individual family members. For another, transferences and countertransferences are always present, but are "diluted" when working with family units (p. 147). Also, trying to assume the parental role is problematic. There are also significant advantages in working with family units; for example, using an individual therapist for each family member is unnecessary if the family is treated as an emotional unit.

CONCLUSIONS

This section reviews the emergence of the theory and clinical practice of family psychotherapy in the Family Study Project.

Centrality of theory. Bowen focused on theory before and throughout the Family Study Project. Theory guided the initial conceptualization and treatment of the mother–daughter dyads. Based on observations, when it became apparent that the entire family was involved, the theory was extended to include the family unit and the treatment was altered accordingly. Theory influenced methods of practice in the change from an individual focus to the family as an emotional unit. While family psychotherapy captured the curiosity and excitement of project visitors, the theoretical underpinnings of this method were probably missed.

Family psychotherapy. Family psychotherapy was developed as a method of working with family units. This particular method offered beneficial aspects for the staff. The family groups were successful as follows:

> for dealing with daily family problems without someone getting and staying over identified, over protective, or over involved with a single family member. The group does not prevent involvements. It offers a way of seeing them clearly. (Bowen, 2013, p. 54)

The group was also therapeutic because the problems presented to the group could be resolved within each family unit.

Now that we have a historical overview of Bowen's study project and the shifts in therapeutic theory that it created, I will focus in chapter 5 on the structure of family psychotherapy theory as elaborated in Bowen's own published papers.

Chapter Five

Bowen's NIMH Family Study Project and the Origins of Family Psychotherapy[2]

Bowen's NIMH project, the 3-East Family Study, was an innovative research effort conducted from November 1954 to December 1958. The original purpose was a study of the nature of symbiosis in mother–daughter dyads where the child was diagnosed with schizophrenia. Bowen's interest in symbiosis developed during his training and subsequent clinical practice at Menninger's (Kerr & Bowen, 1988). During the first year of the Family Study Project, mother and daughter dyads lived on a research unit and were observed for long periods of time, often for more than a year. The criterion for acceptance in the research project was based on the severity of symbiosis rather than the degree of emotional symptoms of the child. Later in the study fathers and "normal" siblings of the schizophrenic patient were included.

The Family Study Project produced many noteworthy findings. One central discovery, based on long-term observational data, was the formulation of a new perspective where the family was conceptualized as an emotional unit. This concept became one cornerstone of Bowen family systems theory. Closely related to this idea was the development of family psychotherapy, a method of treatment for the family unit and as one solution to the management of emotional intensity in project families and staff. During the Family Study Project, the traditional therapeutic relationship was replaced with a new therapeutic role based on the family psychotherapy method. Far from being outdated, Bowen's Family Study Project findings offer important contributions to today's clinical challenges of managing the emotionality of self in clinical practice.

This paper seeks to accomplish several purposes. Based on a research proposal to the National Library of Medicine, 17 unpublished annual summaries, project description sheets, unpublished papers, and presentations from the Family Study Project are reviewed in light of specific questions. First, what factors contributed to the development of family psychotherapy? Second, what facilitated the shift from a conventional therapeutic relationship to a new therapeutic role with project families? These interrelated processes will now be discussed.

CRITICAL FACTORS IN THE DEVELOPMENT
OF FAMILY PSYCHOTHERAPY

Ongoing Challenges in Managing Symbiosis

The Family Study Project was originally designed to study symbiosis in mother–daughter dyads. The initial report was written in December 1954, two months after the project began (Bowen, 2013). The project began with two mother–daughter dyads with a third pair added in early 1955 (Bowen, 2013). The second interim report was written in May 1955. The very first project observation was that staff tensions were "formidable" and that these "seriously threatened" the project structure (Bowen, 1955a). The tensions referred to the difficulty of the staff in daily management of the intensities of the project families. A project description sheet, written 14 months after the project began, noted there was an awareness of the importance of "an ever increasing respect for the difficulties of getting a staff together and welding it into a smooth working unit capable of dealing with a problem of this intensity" (Bowen, 2013, p. 25). Adapting an inpatient unit for families was a very unusual practice at that time. A project report concluded the symbiosis in the dyads had the ability of shifting conflicts to the staff and causing a disturbance between them and that techniques were being developed to help contain the conflicts within the families (Bowen, 1956a).

A project formulation completed in July 1956 is the longest and most detailed concerning inherent difficulties in developing and maintaining transference relationships with psychotic patients and their families (Bowen, 2013). It is the most comprehensive summary of Bowen's thinking on this issue in the project papers. Bowen determined that the transference with psychotic patients was different than with neurotic patients and that it took significant skill and training to work successfully with these intense relationships. The goal was to keep the transference "on the level of intensity of neurotic transference" (Bowen, 2013, p. 47). The plan was to have the "immature symbiotic sides of both the patient and mother could stay contained within the two of them" (p. 47). In actuality, it was not that easy. The mother–daughter symbiosis "tended to get stuck to ward staff" (p. 49). "This kind of helplessness is a very sticky thing . . . and it is easy for it to attach itself to protective mothering or firm direction" (pp. 49–50).

The annual project report in 1956 continued to comment on numerous incidents where the families placed the anxiety upon staff, resulting in the families being calmer but the staff becoming upset (Bowen, 2013). But, if the staff could be calmer and more objective, then so could the families. Controlling intra-staff tensions helped to clearly recognize family difficulties (Bowen, 2013). Ongoing staff training in this critical area was a priority.

Each year of the project it was the goal that the staff develop an effective method to address the emotional problems of the project families (Bowen, 1957a). The intensity of emotional conflicts between the family members was unanticipated in the original research plan.

THE CONCEPT OF THE FAMILY AS AN EMOTIONAL UNIT

The concept of the family as an emotional unit is widely recognized as one of the foundational concepts in Bowen's theory (Bowen, 1978; Kerr & Bowen, 1988). This concept originated very early in the Family Study Project (Bowen, 2013).

The first mention of the importance of other family members, that is, fathers, was mentioned in a project description sheet in December 1955, 14 months after the study began (Bowen, 2013). In the section on the proposed course of the project, there is the first reference to a "shift" from seeing schizophrenia as an illness in a patient perhaps influenced by the mother, to a new perspective of viewing schizophrenia as a product of a distressed family that gets focused on one person (Bowen, 1955). The direction of the project was changed to a "family project" versus a "mother–patient" project. This dates the beginning of the concept of the family as an emotional system. The title of the next report clearly reflected this change: "A Study of Family Relationships in Schizophrenia" (Bowen, 1956a). The basic hypothesis was revised:

> In summary then, the conceptual assumption is that psychosis is more than a problem within one person, that the nucleus of the problem is in a symbiotic relationship with the mother, and that the quality and intensity of the symbiotic relationship is influenced by certain other family relationships. (p. 2)

Bowen (1957a, 1957c) acknowledged that the efforts to conceive of the family as an emotional unit were due to clinical challenges.

> Many decisions that affected the entire course were fortuitous ones to deal with the emotional emergency of the moment. Such was the decision to put the

entire family together into family unit psychotherapy. Originally conceived as an emergency measure to control uncontrolled emotion, it opened up a new area of observations, techniques and concepts. (Bowen, 1957b, p. 11)

If the staff related to individuals, it increased the chances that the family problem could become an intra-staff problem. However, the "family unit" concept made it possible for the staff to view the family in a different way and provided a different view of psychosis that was absent in other approaches (Bowen, 1958a).

In the *Prospectus*, written at the conclusion of the project for a foundation grant that was never obtained, Bowen (2013) noted that the conceptual shift from the individual to the family unit involved three steps: first to think in terms of the family rather than the individual; second, for the staff to relate to the family as a unit; and third, to treat the family psychotherapeutically as a single unit. Bowen (2013) concluded that the concept of "the family as a unit" was the primary finding of the Family Study Project. The "Prospectus" is the best summary of the Family Study Project that I have found.

THE ORIGINS OF FAMILY PSYCHOTHERAPY
AND A NEW THERAPEUTIC ROLE

Initially each member of the dyad was offered individual psychotherapy, which was the accepted practice at that time. Specifically, a psychiatrist saw the patient while the clinical social worker saw the mother. Nursing, occupational therapy, and medical care were also offered to each person (Bowen, 1955).

A combination patient–staff/family council began as a remedy to contain the anxiety within each family unit and to prevent symbiosis from attaching to the staff. Each family was treated as a group, not as a collection of individuals. The treatment philosophy was "to be helpful while staying detached from the other person's immaturities" (Bowen, 1955, p. 9). The ideal therapeutic course was to shift the focus from the patient to the parents. The assumption was that if the parents began to change, so would the patient.

Later in the project, Bowen, Dysinger, Brodey, and Basamania (1957) noted that the individual psychotherapy for both mothers and daughters overall was not that successful. "It appeared that the therapy had attenuated the intensity of the symbiosis, but the pattern was still there. Mother and patient were still completely invested in each other" (p. 8).

The goal was to develop a method to keep the symbiosis within the family group (Bowen, 1956a). Many were tried but only one seemed to hold promise. This was the establishment of daily patient–staff groups or family councils, first mentioned in 1956. These groups served the following functions: reducing instances of patients getting into intense one-to-one relationships with staff, helping family members be more mature, and assisting with staff overinvolvement. These daily groups were so successful that all individual psychotherapy was discontinued. This development of psychotherapy for the family was the result of "clinical necessity" to assist in the management of symbiosis (Bowen, 1957a). "The group was a means of reducing transferences to a minimum and of keeping the original family relationships intact" (Bowen, 1957d, p. 6). The daily groups did not eliminate the problem of staff overinvolvement, but they did provide a way to recognize it early (Bowen, 1956c).

As the theory moved from dyads to the family as an emotional unit, clinical changes were required. How do you treat the entire family? What should be the therapist's role? With the focus on the family as an emotional unit, a "therapeutic dilemma" was created (Bowen, 1958c); that is, how can a therapeutic relationship develop without the therapist assuming the unreal position of a parent? Bowen's (1958c) solution was to return the patient to their family, leaving the therapist in a position of less involvement and more objectivity. Bowen (1958c) was also careful to draw distinctions between group therapy and treating the family as a unit with family psychotherapy. The goal of family therapy became "the analysis of already existing intense interdependent relationships within the family and to analyze them 'in situ' rather than to permit 'transfer' to the relationship with the therapist" (Bowen, 1958c, p. 2).

Conclusions and General Observations

The seeds of coaching as it is known today were sown in the Family Study Project. The first finding about the challenge of symbiosis necessitated the development of a method to effectively manage this problem. If symbiosis was a problem with two or three dyads, the difficultly increased exponentially when entire families were admitted. One reason smaller family units were recruited, that is, parents, symptomatic children, and nonsymptomatic siblings, was to make this problem more manageable. Symbiosis was viewed as a family process.

The staff–patient groups, later known as family psychotherapy, were developed as a means to manage the intensity of the family unit and reflected the theoretical move from the individual to the concept of the family as an emotional unit. It was the problem of managing symbiosis that forced a search for a solution, and the concept of the family as a unit provided the answer. A last conclusion is that the Family Study Project demonstrated that it was not necessary to foster a transference relationship to work effectively with the project families.

Finally, some general observations concerning the documents: First, the "family as an emotional unit" concept and family psychotherapy with a new therapeutic role were not brief experiments; these concepts were utilized for the last three years of the project. Second, there is minimal use of psychiatric terminology in the papers. Bowen sought to describe complex family processes in straightforward language. Third, while there was frequent mention of an outpatient program, so far I have found no papers on this subject. The outpatients, however, did offer a useful comparison group with families with similar problems but less intensity. Fourth, from the onset the Family Study Project was conceptually/theoretically driven. For example, there was initially a theoretical conceptualization of the problem, that is, a reciprocal intense mother–daughter attachment that produced symptoms in both. Later this theoretical assumption was revised to view psychosis as more than a problem within just one individual. Fifth, the papers offer valuable insights about symbiosis in families, a process that is alive and well in families today. Last, the basic elements of coaching today were present in the Family Study Project. The coach works to address their emotional functioning, lets the family be responsible for problems, works to make emotional contact with family members, and makes observations about family process.

Now that I have reviewed Murray Bowen's outlining of his new family systems psychotherapy theory and guidance for clinical practice, I will delve a bit more deeply in the next chapter into the fundamental concept of the family as an emotional unit.

Chapter Six

The Family-as-a-Unit Concept and the Therapeutic Relationship

The previous two chapters highlighted the background, development, and central findings concerning Bowen's NIMH Family Study Project. A key finding of that innovative research effort is the concept of the family as an emotional unit. Bowen provides a broad definition of the family: "the total number of individuals attached to an emotional nucleus" (Kerr, 1998, p. 132). This definition takes into account the wide diversity of family configurations.

The concept of the family as an emotional unit provides a cornerstone for Bowen's other theoretical concepts and also redefines the nature of the therapeutic relationship. The concept became entwined with the origin and development of family psychotherapy, the second seminal finding of the Family Study Project. While it is acknowledged that differentiation of self is "the" cornerstone of Bowen family systems theory, buildings can have several cornerstones.

The objective of this chapter is to demonstrate the importance of the concept of the family as an emotional unit in the therapeutic relationship. Specific goals for this chapter include:

1. Addressing the implications of the concept of the family as an emotional unit for the therapeutic relationship. Guided by the triadic model, the word *therapeutic relationship* will be used rather than the current term *therapeutic alliance* or simply *the alliance*. The triadic model divides the therapeutic relationship into three overlapping parts: the alliance, transference and countertransference, and the real relationship (Meissner, 2000).
2. Reviewing how this concept anchors the therapeutic relationship in a broader perspective.
3. Highlighting the details of how the concept guides the therapeutic relationship.

4. Examining how this concept focuses and orients the process of clinical assessment.
5. Exploring how the intensity of transferences is reduced when working with family emotional units.
6. Outlining several challenges for both therapists and family members in the application of the concept.

IMPLICATIONS OF THE CONCEPT OF THE FAMILY AS AN EMOTIONAL UNIT

In my view, the individual model rather than a family systems model has been the dominant perspective in clinical practice and research. This model continues to provide useful research about the biology, psychology, and psychosocial functioning of the individual. The fifth revision of the *Diagnostic and Statistical Manual of Mental Disorders* (*DSM-V*) is still primarily focused on the diagnosis of the individual rather than the symptomatic person in the crucible of their nuclear and extended families. The family system model provides an alternative way of thinking about the emotional functioning of people in the context of their most important family relationships.

Bowen concluded during the first year of his research project that the mother–daughter dyads living in the Family Project facilities were just a small part of a larger emotional system involving other important family members such as fathers and siblings. His term was that the dyad was a "fragment" of the entire family (Bowen, 1978, p. 24). In another significant finding, he concluded that one important treatment goal should be to avoid the psychological symbiosis rather than embracing it directly. This effort proved to be a considerable challenge for the staff, however. It was of course the direct opposite of the clinical practice at the time. Both then and now clinicians have underestimated the intense emotionality in therapeutic situations and overestimated their ability to manage these emotions.

Just what are some important implications of viewing the family as an emotional unit? The first is the principle of reciprocity or the interdependence of emotional functioning; those around us influence our behavior and we in turn influence them. It is always a system of mutual interactions.

Second is recognizing the existence of predictable behavioral patterns in human families in their management of anxiety. These patterns were recognized and detailed during the Family Study Project. In one of Bowen's important unpublished papers, "The Prospectus," he highlighted some of these clinical patterns (Bowen, 2013, p. 153). One example is overfunctioning in relationships where one partner overfunctions and the other underfunctions. This pattern may play out in families, work settings, or social relationship systems. Bowen recognized the importance of the idea of reciprocity in relationships, which is the principle behind over- and under-functioning. You cannot have an overfunctioning person in a family without having someone who also underfunctions. Many times the reciprocity in relationships is not recognized; instead the spotlight is on the person who underfunctions with some type of symptom. In addition to Bowen, several early researchers also recognized these family patterns but used different terms to describe them (Wynne, 1958).

Third, if the family is conceptualized as an emotional unit, then people have less emotional control than they think. Those around us influence our behavior; it is a system of continual emotional interactions.

Finally, if the proposition is accepted that the family is an emotional unit, then the assessment of the individual is incomplete if the social and emotional functioning of the nuclear and extended families is ignored. Fortunately, another of Bowen's early developments was a graphic method to highlight the emotional processes and functioning in the multigenerational family. This method is called the "family diagram," and it provides an unparalleled perspective on the multigenerational family. The family diagram is also known as a *genogram*.

THE CONCEPT OF THE FAMILY AS AN EMOTIONAL UNIT AS ANCHOR FOR THE THERAPEUTIC RELATIONSHIP

Family research has identified some characteristics of emotional systems that put the therapeutic relationship into a broader perspective. (Bowen, 1978, p. 342)

An overview of Bowen's thinking about the therapeutic relationship is found in his classic text, *Family Therapy in Clinical Practice*, originally published in 1978. In a section of chapter 16 titled "Theory in the Practice of Psychotherapy," Bowen carefully outlines his thoughts on how the therapeutic relationship can be placed in a broader perspective.

Bowen determined that when the family is viewed as an emotional unit, the therapeutic relationship is in fact placed into a broader perspective. The broader lens results from an orientation toward the family as an emotional unit, which is significantly different than the traditional therapist–patient relationship. Ideally, the therapist relates to the family unit regardless of who is present in the consulting room. Most people live and die in family emotional units rather than in isolation. Both humans and nonhuman primates tend to live their lives in relationship to their larger multigenerational families.

Bowen begins with a discussion regarding the impact on a family when a "significant other," such as a therapist, begins his/her clinical work with a family. Structural family therapists have used the term "joining with the family," to describe when a therapist first enters a family. Bowen proposed that the mere entry of a therapist into an anxious family system alters family emotional processes. Also, when a patient becomes involved in individual psychotherapy, his/her family can calm down. It is as if the anxiety is drained from the family unit and then absorbed by the therapist–patient relationship. However, as the individual therapist–patient relationship becomes more intense, the patient may distance from his/her family and into the therapeutic relationship, which over time can have a negative impact on the family.

When the therapist becomes involved with an individual or family he/she instantly becomes a significant other with "assumed, assigned or actual" status (Bowen, 1978, p. 345). In addition, if multiple therapists become involved with a family, which is a common practice today, the situation can become even more complicated. Bowen thought the emotionality of the therapeutic relationship in psychotherapy tended to be on "the high side" compared to other types of professional relationships (Bowen, 1978, p. 345). And in certain types of therapeutic relationships such as psychoanalysis, where the development and exploration of transferences is encouraged and explored, the intensity of the patient–therapist relationship is very high. One significant finding, often overlooked during Bowen's NIMH project, moved him away from conventional psychoanalytic theory and treatment toward a family systems approach. This was during the first year when Bowen and his colleagues observed that working 24 hours a day, 7 days a week with the inpatient families was both very emotionally intense and a major challenge for the staff. It was a significant test for the staff not to be overinvolved or have alternating overinvolvements with individual family members. In fact, this emotional intensity and staff overinvolvement was so problematic that it threatened the very existence of the project. This was a clinical and administrative problem that had to be quickly and effectively resolved. The resolution for overinvolvement was found in family psychotherapy.

THE CONCEPT OF THE FAMILY AS AN EMOTIONAL UNIT AS A GUIDE TO THE THERAPEUTIC ROLE

The change to family research provided a new dimension for dealing with the therapeutic relationship. It became theoretically possible to leave the intensity of the relationship between the original family members, and bypass some of the time-consuming detail. (Bowen, 1978, p. 346)

The concept of the family as an emotional unit provides clarity about the functions of the therapeutic role. The central guidance is provided by the theoretical orientation of this concept as well as other related concepts. If one can accept the idea of the family an emotional unit, then the focus of therapy must be on that multigenerational family as a unit and not just on a group of individuals or an individual patient.

But how is the therapeutic relationship directed? Is it a dyad or a larger system view? Family systems theory provides a theoretical template for thinking about these clinical issues. At the inception of the NIMH Family Study Project, Bowen's theory concerned the psychological symbiosis between mother–child dyads. During the first year, however, it became apparent that the mothers and daughters were just "a fragment" of a larger emotional system that involved others significant to that dyad (Bowen, 1988, p. 24). Fathers and the siblings of the patient were then included in the project. Thus, the initial theory focusing on the psychological symbiosis in the dyad was extended to highlight this process in the family as a whole.

What exactly is guided by theory? Primarily it is the thinking of the therapist. Theory is seen as critical in the conduct of clinical practice. Is it the focus on the symptomatic person and how the family should care for the member who is ill, or is it the focus on the family as a unit where one member is symptomatic? It is not the number of people in the consulting room but the theory that the therapist uses that is important.

Clinical practice flows from the theory, and a number of approaches to clinical practice follow. If one accepts that the family is an emotional unit, then the treatment must be on that unit. In addition, the importance of the therapeutic relationship is significantly reduced, and the emphasis falls on finding and nurturing family leaders and coaching family members to increase contact with their family.

The concept of triangles is also important in the therapeutic relationship. The triangle is one of Bowen's eight interlocking theoretical concepts. Triangles are viewed as the basic molecule of the family. Furthermore, if one can be a neutral third person and relate to an anxious twosome, the two others will be calmer. A triangle exists when a therapist consults with a couple. The neutral posture and viable emotional contact in the presence of an anxious twosome is more significant than what is said by the clinician.

THE CONCEPT OF THE FAMILY AS AN EMOTIONAL UNIT AS FOCUS FOR CLINICAL ASSESSMENT

The published and unpublished papers concerning the Family Study Project make clear that Bowen's concept of the family as an emotional unit and family psychotherapy are inexorably intertwined (Bowen, 2013). Family psychotherapy was derived as one method to work with family units. In addition, family psychotherapy was effective in highlighting and reducing staff overinvolvements and in placing the emotional intensity into the family unit rather than the therapeutic relationship.

If the focus is on the family unit, then the unit must be evaluated. There is certainly nothing wrong with the traditional individual mental health evaluations of children, adolescents, or adults; however, it is also essential to understand the multigenerational context of these individuals.

A method of evaluating the facts of family units was developed during the Family Study Project. Called the *family diagram*, it was first used by Bowen and his colleagues in the project to record facts about the multigenerational family. Since then, the details and specifics of family diagrams have been more fully developed. This method of assessing family emotional units calls for certain details about each member of the nuclear and extended family: What has been their functioning? What are the physical, emotional, and social symptoms of each person in the nuclear and extended families?

IS IT POSSIBLE TO "DILUTE" TRANSFERENCES BY FOCUSING ON FAMILY EMOTIONAL UNITS?

> But Bowen kept one Freudian concept. I once asked him about the phenomenon of transference. He said, "I don't see how you can get around it." (Gilbert, 2011, p. 7)

Bowen did not discard the concepts of transference and countertransference. He did not, however, accept their theoretical underpinnings. In fact, Bowen replaced the early Freudian concept of the unconscious with his concept of the emotional system (Kerr, 2013). While his published writings contain no articles focusing exclusively on these concepts, he did discuss them generally. One example is located in his archives and was recently published (Bowen, 2013). The title of this paper in chapter 3 (p. 43) is "Formulation of 3 East Family Study Project July 26, 1956: The Treatment of Schizophrenia Using Modifications of Psychoanalytic Techniques and Extension of Psychoanalytic Theory." The paper is a seminal document and worth a careful reading. In this paper, Bowen proposed that it is possible to reduce the intensity of transferences when working with chronically ill patients and their families.

In working with intense emotional reactions with project families, Bowen noticed that the staff who were able to manage their emotionality also had the best control over their countertransference reactions. The staff's automatic reactions were a major issue in the Family Study Project. The project families were experts in involving staff in their problems.

In a significant departure from conventional psychoanalytic practice, Bowen advocated a new position for the therapeutic relationship. Rather than embracing and interpreting the emotionality displayed by the families, Bowen and his colleagues worked diligently to avoid emotionality within the family. The goal was to let the family handle the emotionality. He wrote, "operationally, the 'symbiotic sides' of both patients and daughters tended to stick to ward staff. . . . This kind of helplessness is a very sticky thing as we see it, and it is easy for it to attach itself to protective mothering or firm direction" (Bowen, 2013, pp. 49–50). In other words, the goal was to *contain* the emotionality within the family unit rather than within the patient–therapist relationship. But it was not an easy task then, and it is still not easy to work toward placing the immaturity back into the family.

In answer to the question posed at the beginning of this section, it is possible that "transference and countertransference are present in therapy with the family unit but can be diluted" (Basamania, 2013, p. 147). Basamania's article was prepared for a workshop in 1959 and later published in the *Journal of Orthopsychiatry* in 1961. In addition, Bowen found that "the group was a means of reducing transferences to a minimum and of keeping the original family relationships intact" (Bowen, 2013, p. 22). The "group" referred to the daily family groups in the project.

So, if one works with the family emotional system, it is possible to reduce but not eliminate transference reactions. The topics of transference and countertransference are not written about with great frequency in Bowen family systems literature. Often other terms such as *automatic reactivity* (Gilbert, 1992) are used to describe these processes. Such a term does not have the particular theoretical implication of the *transference*. Kerr (1988) also notes that working in this manner does not replicate troublesome unresolved emotional attachments that the patient has to his/her parents. An important finding from the Family Project was that it is not necessary to enhance and interpret transferences in order to help families change.

CHALLENGES IN APPLYING THE CONCEPT OF THE FAMILY AS AN EMOTIONAL UNIT

Challenges for Clinicians

Each clinician with a primary orientation to family systems theory and its applications must find his/her own way to represent the family system perspective to family members. In the face of the preeminence of the individual orientation, this is not an easy task.

Bowen outlined early in his project papers the significant challenges presented to the clinician who works to embrace fully the concept of the family as an emotional unit and the types of awareness needed to conduct family unit–oriented therapy: intellectual, clinical, and emotional.

The first step in conducting family unit–oriented therapy is to establish an intellectual awareness of the concept. Many readers have taken the familiar multiple-choice exams in undergraduate and/or graduate school. For example, is the family as an emotional unit most often identified with (a) Bowen, (b) Freud, (c) Minchin, or (d) Goolishian and Anderson? Many can master an intellectual awareness of the concept.

The second step involves a clinical awareness of this concept. Some people have an intellectual understanding of the concept but have great difficulty applying it clinically. The therapist may also mix individual and family therapy in his/her clinical approaches depending on who is in the room. It is clearly more difficult to apply the concept and assess its ramifications in clinical situations.

Third, the therapist must have an emotional awareness of the concept. How does the therapist shift from an individual orientation psychopathology to an emotional awareness of the family as an emotional unit? Bowen (1978, p. 74) spoke of the process of shifting "emotional detachment" from the individual to the family emotional unit as a necessary ability in this process.

Challenges for Individuals, Couples, and Families

It is not always easy for parents to hear that in fact their child's emotional difficulties may relate to problems within the family. In fact, some cannot hear this. This idea has to be presented with a non-blaming posture. The families in Bowen's project would not have stayed long if they felt blamed and accused. Each therapist operating from a family systems theory approach must find a way of representing these concepts to individuals, couples, and families (Bowen, 1978). I have found one question suggested by one of my coaches useful to ask a parent or parents: "Can you *entertain* the idea that the child's behavior may be related to events in the family?" (Dan Papero, personal communication, 2008). The response is diagnostic and can determine the course of treatment.

Parents, for example, present with definite thinking about the nature and origin of clinical problems. They may think the child has "a chemical imbalance" or has been diagnosed with ADHD. The problem then resides totally within the child. They are frustrated and often are in a helpless position. When parents say to me, "I've tried everything and nothing works," it is a clear indication of a helpless stance. Another signal of helplessness is when parents say that their child "needs someone to talk to." The translation—they are helpless and want me to "fix their child."

SUMMARY

During and after the NIMH Family Study Project, Bowen argued for a very different therapeutic role than that existed then or exists today. He did not believe that the usual term of "therapeutic relationship" accurately described this new role. So, he proposed other terms such as *coaching* or *supervising* to better articulate his method of clinical work. Unfortunately, the term "coaching" he used in the past is associated presently with "executive" or "life" coaching, which is much different than Bowen's original use of the term. Over time, the term Bowen thought would clearly delineate his version of the therapeutic relationship has been confused with other terms.

Viewing the family as an emotional unit has many important implications. Overall, the concept provides an alternative way of thinking about clinical problems. In addition, the concept gives clarity/direction to the therapeutic relationship. That is, if the therapeutic relationship is based on the concept of the family being viewed as an emotional unit, then the therapeutic relationship is in fact placed in a broader perspective since the family is seen as the patient even if only one member has symptoms. Family systems theory then is critical in the conduct of therapy and for the personal growth and development of the therapist. One of the eight interlocking theoretical constructs is that of triangles. It is important to understand how triangles operate in the clinical situation.

The concept of the family as an emotional unit also provides specific guidance for assessment. It is the family unit that falls under the clinician's microscope. In addition, to graphically display facts of functioning and emotional processes in families, the family diagram has been developed.

Working or viewing individuals in the context of their multigenerational family is highly beneficial because working with these family units can "dilute" transferences. Far from being easy and straightforward to apply, challenges/obstacles exist for both the therapist and family members.

Now that the implications of using the concept of the family as a unit have been explained and applied to clinical practice, in the next chapter I will outline the relationship between the tripartite model of the therapeutic relationship and family systems theory.

Chapter Seven

The Tripartite Model of the Therapeutic Relationship and Family Systems Theory

TRADITIONAL PERSPECTIVES

Gelso individually and with his colleagues has been consistent in his definition of the therapeutic relationship. The original definition, used in an article (Gelso & Carter, 1985), has been repeated in follow-up publications. They defined the therapeutic relationship as "the feelings and attitudes that the counseling participants have toward one another and the manner in which these are expressed" (p. 159).

From a psychoanalytic perspective, Meissner's view is that the "components of the therapeutic relationship include transference and its correlative, countertransference, the real relationship, and the therapeutic alliance" (Meissner, 1999, p. 1). He further notes that these components continually interact and represent the elements of all therapeutic relationships regardless of orientation or discipline.

FAMILY SYSTEMS THEORY PERSPECTIVES

Bowen. Murray Bowen is perhaps most identified with a natural family systems theory bearing his name that includes eight interlocking concepts. These concepts are nuclear family emotional processes, the family projection process, multigenerational transmission, triangles, sibling position, emotional cutoff, and differentiation of self and societal emotional processes.

Bowen developed natural family systems theory in alignment with the principles of evolution and the viewpoint that humans are the product of evolution. His definition of family systems theory and therapy was "a combination of the family as seen through the lens of some Freud, plus evolution,

69

integrated by natural systems theory" (Kerr & Bowen, 1988, p. 383). In my view, *family* refers to conceptualizing the family as an emotionally interdependent unit. This is the central finding of his NIMH project. The "some Freud" indicates Bowen's respect and for use of Freud's concepts of neutrality and transference and countertransference and how these apply to families. The term *evolution* reflects Bowen's broad view of mankind as a part of all living things, whereas *integrated by natural systems theory* refers to Bowen theory's eight interlocking concepts. Thus, family systems theory and therapy form a distinctive approach with applications beyond psychotherapy in areas such as business, religion, and personal development.

In *Family Therapy in Clinical Practice*, Bowen devoted a long section in one chapter to the topic of therapeutic relationship with the goal of contrasting his work with other methods of psychotherapy. Actually, in his writings, lectures, and videos, Bowen distanced himself from the term *therapeutic relationship*. He wanted to make clear how his thinking on this topic differed significantly from other psychotherapy models.

Bowen thought that the therapeutic roles in family psychotherapy and coaching were much different from other psychotherapy methods. For example, family psychotherapy implies a primary emphasis on treating the family as an emotional unit rather than working primarily within a therapist–patient dyad. The practice of family psychotherapy originated in Bowen's NIMH project, where therapists first worked with family units.

In 1970, Bowen introduced the role of a coach in his paper "From Couch to Coach." This paper describes the evolution of his thinking about different approaches to working with families and individuals. Initially Bowen was trained in psychoanalytic psychotherapy while at the Menninger Clinic from 1946 to 1954. Following his time in the Family Study Project (1954–1959), he became a clinical professor in the Department of Psychiatry at Georgetown Medical School before moving off campus and forming the Georgetown Family Center in 1975. Initially Bowen thought that psychoanalysis should be the primary method for the treatment of emotional difficulties. Following his research project, he recommended family psychotherapy for the clinician and their spouse as a more effective method of treatment. Later, a method to supplement family psychotherapy was introduced. Here the therapist functioned as a teacher about how emotional systems functioned in families and as a *coach* when the patient worked outside the office in applying this knowledge with his/her parental family (Bowen, 1970). Just what are some of the differences between coaching and a traditional therapeutic alliance? And what are the seminal aspects of coaching?

Family psychotherapy and later coaching are intertwined within family systems theory and its eight interlocking concepts. If one embraces the concept that the family is an emotional unit, then this concept guides the therapist's assessment and treatment approaches as well as his/her actions in session regardless of who is in the consulting room. The therapeutic role focuses on the multigenerational family rather than on a person with symptoms. Furthermore, the therapeutic goal is to obtain a position outside the family emotional processes rather than becoming involved in them.

Family psychotherapy works to direct emotionality back into the family unit rather than into a dyadic therapist–patient relationship. Said another way, the patient uses his/her own family to address unresolved emotional issues rather than using the therapeutic relationship (Bowen, 2013). The therapist also works diligently to minimize involvement in the family's emotionality as opposed to managing this in a therapeutic relationship. Bowen initially called this *emotional nonparticipation*; today it is known as emotional neutrality (Kerr & Bowen, 1988).

When the family psychotherapist takes the position of an observer with the family and directs emotionality back into the family, this creates a psychological void. Bowen termed this a *therapeutic dilemma* (Bowen, Brodey, Dysinger, & Basamania, 1959). On one hand, patients seem to need a person in the traditional therapist's role. If this therapeutic relationship is altered, then who will fill this void? Bowen's answer was that it should be the patient's own family. Bowen thought that the patient's family should be seen as a major resource for him/her rather than having the therapeutic relationship be that resource.

THE ALLIANCE

Traditional Perspectives

Gelso. Gelso and Carter (1994) defined the working alliance as "the alignment or joining together of the reasonable self or ego of the client and the therapist's analyzing or 'therapizing' side for the purpose of the work" (p. 297).

Meissner. Meissner (2006) views the therapeutic alliance as including "all those factors and dimensions of the analytic relation that constitute the therapeutic pact and determine the context within which effective therapeutic interventions, interactions, and interpretative communication can take place" (p. 265).

Bordin. Bordin (1979) wrote a highly influential transtheoretical paper on the concept of the working alliance. His influence helped unify the theory in this area and enhanced empirical research on the alliance as well. In his 1979 paper, Bordin proposed "that the working alliance between the person who seeks change and the one who offers to be a change agent is one of the keys, if not the key, to the change process" (p. 252). Furthermore, Bordin (1979) determined that the "working alliance includes three features: an agreement on goals, as assignment of tasks or a series of tasks, and the development of bonds" (p. 253). Researchers in individual and family psychotherapy continue to use Bordin's conceptual framework as the basis for the development of alliance measures.

Horvath. Building on the theoretical work of Bordin, Horvath and Greenburg (1989) provided details on the development and validation of the Working Alliance Inventory (WAI), an early alliance measure. The WAI is the only alliance measure based entirely on Bordin's formulation. Horvath has spent a great deal of his professional career on the areas of alliance theory and measurement. Based on Bordin's alliance formulation, Horvath and Greenburg (1989) describe the development, clinical trials, reliability, and validity of the WAI. Since the concept of the therapeutic alliance may be an important vehicle of change in psychotherapy, the WAI is one effort to help quantify this variable. The WAI, which has both therapist and client versions, has become one of the most popular measures of the therapeutic alliance and continues to be utilized in many research studies.

In an earlier article, noting that some authors use the terms *alliance* and *therapeutic relationship* synonymously, Horvath (2001) provides his definition of the therapeutic alliance:

> The alliance refers to the quality and strength of the collaborative relationship between client and therapist in therapy. This concept is inclusive of: the positive affective bonds between client and therapist, such as mutual trust, liking, respect and caring. Alliance also encompasses the more cognitive aspects of the therapy relationship; consensus about, and active commitment to, the goals of therapy and to the means by which these goals can be reached. Alliance involves a sense of partnership in therapy between therapist and client, in which each participant is actively committed to their specific and appropriate responsibilities in therapy, and believes the other is likewise enthusiastically engaged in the process. The alliance is a conscious and purposeful aspect of the relation between therapist and client. (p. 36)

Family Systems Perspectives

Bowen. Bowen (1978) viewed the alliance as an intense form of the therapeutic relationship. In family systems theory, working toward viable emotional contact with the individual or individuals in the consulting room is the goal of the coach or family psychotherapist. An alliance is seen as possibly having too much emotionality within the therapist–patient relationship.

Except in the family therapy literature where the focus is on multiple alliances, much of the attention about the alliance remains on therapist–patient dyads. Bowen's clinical direction is on the family as an emotional unit, which is a broader perspective. One traditional assumption is that a strong therapist–patient dyad is necessary to a positive outcome; however, it is also possible to consciously work to minimize the emotional intensity in psychotherapy and still have positive clinical outcomes.

Bowen was acutely aware of this challenge of emotionality early in his NIMH family project. A close reading of his papers written during the project, now available for study, demonstrates the difficulties all staff faced in personally managing the intense emotions while working with the project families (Bowen, 2013). This emotionality resulted from the intense psychological symbiosis within and between the families and staff. The choice was either to absorb emotionality within a therapeutic relationship or to find ways to reduce it. Bowen and his colleagues went in the direction of working to minimize the emotionality.

One effective means to accomplish this was to view the patient as the family unit and relate to the family unit as a whole. Another was to have the patient's family take more responsibility for the patient. An alternative view about therapist–patient relationships is highlighted in his early project papers (Bowen, 2013) and concerned the concept of maturity and immaturity. Bowen viewed the therapist and the patient as having mature and immature sides; he represented these with a circle divided in half, one half representing the mature side and the other half the immature side. Bowen thought that is was easy for the patient to show his/her immature side to the therapist. The challenge was for the therapist not to respond with his/her immature side but with their mature side. In addition, the goal was for the patient's mature side to manage their immaturity rather than have the therapist be responsible for this.

Bowen's perspective on this area was as follows:

> One of our goals in family psychotherapy is to leave the already existing relationship within the family group and to analyze he relationships *in situ* rather than permit transfer to the relationship with the therapist. (Bowen, 1978, p. 29)

Kerr. Michael E. Kerr, MD, was Dr. Bowen's close associate and chief student for many years. Following Dr. Bowen's death in 1990, he became the director of the Georgetown Family Center, now known as the Bowen Center for the Study of the Family. Drs. Kerr and Bowen separately wrote the classic book *Family Evaluation* in 1988.

Kerr has written and presented extensively about Bowen family systems theory and its applications. To this author, one central emphasis of Dr. Kerr's work has been on the concept of differentiation of self, considered the cornerstone of Bowen family systems theory. Related to this is his application on how certain theoretical concepts are universal in all families and are illustrated in the families in the news such of famous people such as Ted Kaczynski, John Nash, and, recently, Adam Lanza.

Kerr has also made significant contributions to the understanding of the role of a coach in family psychotherapy. Within this area, Kerr (1988) emphasized the importance of the training of coaches using differentiation of self. In addition, he stressed focusing on the family psychotherapists' emotional objectivity and neutrality. Questions often arise about the amount of training for coaches with an orientation to family systems theory. Kerr (1981) has suggested that at least three to four years of formal training is appropriate. Such training would involve a program such as the Family Postgraduate Program offered by the Bowen Center. This intensive program meets four times a year for three days with monthly supervision between the sessions. The program is an intensive study of theory and its applications and includes supervision of work in one's family or on clinical cases, issues with one's family of origin or work situations. There are several training programs like this throughout the United States. A major goal of the postgraduate program at the Bowen Center is to become aware and enhance the participant's basic level of differentiation of self.

Another of Dr. Kerr's contributions is his teaching and writing about the three "Es" of Bowen theory, which are useful in family psychotherapy and coaching. The three "Es" are emotional programming, emotional objectivity, and emotional neutrality. Kerr (M. E. Kerr, personal communication, December 2007) defined emotional objectivity as the ability to factually describe the details of emotional systems, and emotional neutrality as the ability to be present a clinical problem but not be overinvolved with the patient and/or family. Kerr also updated and refined Bowen's concept of *emotional detachment*, originally described during and after Bowen's NIMH project, and replaced this term with *emotional neutrality*. Both of these abilities are especially important in clinical work.

Kerr also further elaborated on Bowen's concept of establishing viable emotional contact with family members. He noted:

> My way of interpreting emotional contact is the family members leave a session thinking that you have listened, take an interest in them and their problem, and some understanding of their difficulties. This depends some on being able to imagine what the other is feeling, but also on theory and emotional objectivity. Viable implies to me that the family members believe that they could be helped in such an environment. (M. E. Kerr, personal communication, June 9, 2014)

Papero. Daniel V. Papero, PhD, enjoys a long association with the Bowen Center for the Study of the Family, dating to the 1980s. In 1990, he authored the book, *Bowen Family Systems Theory*. From 1995 to 1997, he was a consultant for clinical social work for the US Air Force. For part of 2015 he was on a sabbatical in Australia, working with clinicians interested in family systems theory.

Dr. Papero, who is a licensed clinical social worker, has made several important contributions to family psychotherapy and coaching processes in Bowen family systems theory. Papero (1990) sees the major effort of the therapist in family systems therapy "to address the thoughtful capacity of the individual as much as possible" (p. 68). One example of this is his question that this author adopted in work with parents. I will ask the parent if they can entertain the idea that the child's problems have something to do with the family. Papero (1990) also introduced the term *research orientation* as an important perspective of the coach (p. 71). This orientation implies a certain cautious, attentive, factual, and investigative role to gather information about the family. Papero views the ideal role of the coach as "gathering information, maintaining a broad perspective, obtaining and maintaining emotional neutrality, and operating from a research perspective" (1990, p. 71).

Papero (2015) provides a recent review of the position of the therapist in family psychotherapy:

> The clinician served as a consultant, supervisor, or coach of the family's effort to move from a position of anxious helplessness to active processes of problem-solving and adaptation to life challenge. Rather than analyzing the individual in the therapeutic hour, as had been the case in psychoanalytic treatment, the clinician worked with the family to assist their analyzing their own relationship processes *in situ* rather than the process between clinician and individual.
>
> The role of consultant or coach required that the clinician avoid intense attachments with any family member. He or she worked to remain aware of one's own emotional responsiveness to the family and regulate that tendency with conscious control. From a position of emotional objectivity and neutrality the clinician could offer observations of the family about the emotional process among them.
>
> The efforts of the clinician assisted the family members to identify or define the problem in the family (not in the individual patient) and then to remain alongside as the family took responsibility for resolving the dilemma. The task for the clinician, as Bowen wrote, was to be helpful without becoming responsible for solving the problem. Family psychotherapy aimed to address the functional helplessness displayed by the family and their attempt to place responsibility for solving the problem outside themselves. When one member can shift his or her part of the family problem and sustain that change, the entire family system can change as well. That is the magic of family psychotherapy. (pp. 27–28)

Gilbert. Roberta Gilbert, MD, is a faculty member at the Bowen Center for the Study of the Family. Her early training as a psychiatrist, however, was in psychoanalytic psychotherapy. Currently she develops and actively participates in a program for the training of clergy members in the theory and practice of family systems therapy.

Gilbert is a prolific writer and has published a number of books in the area of Bowen family systems theory and its applications. These include *Extraordinary Relationships: A New Way of Thinking about Human Interactions* (1992), *Connecting with Our Children: Guiding Principles for Parents in a Troubled World* (1999), *The Eight Concepts of Bowen Theory: A New Way of Thinking about the Individual and the Group* (2004), *Extraordinary Leadership: Thinking Systems, Making a Difference* (2006), and *The Cornerstone Concept* (2008).

Gilbert is also a frequent presenter on the topic of psychotherapy from the perspective of family systems, and parts of her presentations involve the topic of coaching. Gilbert (2004) concludes that psychotherapy guided by Bowen family systems theory involves distinctive features. For example, the lens of family systems theory that the therapist uses to think about clinical problems is critical; the theory used by a therapist influences both assessment and treatment. She also emphasizes the importance of the knowledge of emotional systems and how they work and acceptance of the concept of the family as an emotional unit. In the area of the development of the therapist, knowing family systems theory is a must; if one does not study and know theory, then it is impossible to use the approach clinically and in one's own family. Differentiating a self in one's own family of origin is also a necessity in becoming an effective family systems therapist. Regarding the behaviors of a coach using family systems theory, Gilbert (2008) suggests using any technique that decreases emotionality in sessions, working in managing oneself emotionally, and defining oneself during the clinical hour. Gilbert (1992) concludes by noting "nor is the theory primarily a method for practicing psychotherapy" (p. 9).

Titelman. Peter Titelman, PhD, is a psychologist in private practice in Northampton, Massachusetts. A prolific author and editor, Titelman, has a number of books on the clinical practice of family systems theory and some of the concepts of Bowen theory.

Titelman (1987) noted that the function of a coach in family systems therapy was "to have a neutral relationship with the family, whether a coach seeking to have a neutral relationship with the family, whether meeting with an individual, couple or larger groupings of the nuclear and/or extended family" (p. 21). Titelman (1998) also indicated that one of the most important parts of the therapy process is the emotional functioning of a coach and his/

her own ability to adopt a neutral position when working with emotional systems.

Hargrove. David Hargrove, PhD, is professor emeritus at the University of Mississippi where he was originally the department chair of psychology. He has completed six years in the postgraduate training program at the Bowen Center and is currently on its faculty.

In a recent book chapter on family psychology, Dr. Hargrove writes about the therapeutic relationship in Bowen psychotherapy. Reviewing Bowen's work, Hargrove (2009) notes a critical difference in Bowen psychotherapy from other psychotherapy approaches where "the most important work is done by the patient in relationship to his or her family and not in relationship to the therapist" (p. 9). Hargrove also focuses on having the patient be as objective and thoughtful as possible about his/her nuclear family and family of origin. The role of the therapist must be as neutral as possible and minimize overinvolvement in the emotional processes. Teaching about theory is also important.

This attention to the relationship of the patient and their family changes the roles of both the patient and the therapist compared to traditional psychotherapy. As Hargrove summarizes,

> In psychotherapy based on Bowen theory the patient develops or changes relationships to both nuclear and extended family by making changes in the self. This is done within a "coaching" relationship rather than a healing relationship. The therapist takes on the role of a "coach" by clarifying, making suggestions from the perspective of theory, and assists that patient in the evaluation of the effectiveness of the efforts. (p. 10)

In terms of a concise definition of psychotherapy based on family systems theory, Hargrove offers a comparison to the description of the therapeutic alliance by Gelso and Carter (1985):

> A differentiated self is one who can maintain emotional objectivity while in the midst of an emotional system in turmoil, yet at the same time actively relate to key people in the system. (Bowen, 1978, p. 485)

TRANSFERENCE/COUNTERTRANSFERENCE

Traditional Perspectives

Gelso. "Many see this construct, transference, as Freud's greatest discovery related to psychological treatment" (Gelso, 2014, p. 121). Gelso and Hayes (1998) and Gelso and Bhatia (2012) defined transference as follows: "the patient's experience and perception of the therapist that are shaped by the patient's own psychological structures and past, involving carryover from and displacement onto the therapist of feelings, attitudes, and behaviors belonging rightfully to and in earlier significant relationships" (Gelso, 2014, p. 121).

Gelso and Hayes (2007) defined this concept in the following manner: "the therapist's internal and external reactions that are shaped by the therapist's past and present emotional conflicts and vulnerabilities" (p. 25).

Meissner. According to Meissner (2006a), transference and countertransference "provide the material on which the psychoanalytic process works, not exclusively but in large measure. . . . Psychoanalysis and psychotherapy do not achieve their effects through transference or countertransference but by working in, on, and through them to effectively modify them in more realistic and adaptive directions" (p. 265).

Family Systems Perspectives

Bowen. Bowen retained both the concepts of transference and countertransference in his theory. Gilbert (2011) commented:

> But Bowen kept one Freudian concept. I once asked him about the phenomenon of transference. He said, "I don't see how you can get around it." So automatic responsiveness based on past experience that could interfere, not only with the therapeutic relationship but actually with any relationship, was preserved in the new theory. So also was automaticity in the therapist, countertransference. (p. 6)

However, both historically and today the concepts of transference and countertransference are inexorably bound to psychoanalytic theory and practice and the idea of the unconscious (Kerr & Bowen, 1988). Bowen (1978), however, replaced the concept of the unconscious with the broader concept of an emotional system as the primary force in human behavior. The idea of an emotional system was based on several years of observations during and after his NIMH project (Kerr & Bowen, 1988) and is further clarified as "an intimate part of man's phylogenetic past, which he shares with lower forms of life, and which is governed by the same laws that govern all living things" (Bowen, 1978, p. 197).

Thus, Bowen family systems theory is viewed as a natural systems theory in distinction to other psychotherapy approaches. Bowen's concept of the emotional system provides a foundation for a behavioral link to other species; Darwin also argued for a physical link between man and other forms of life (Kerr & Bowen, 1982). In addition to the emotional system, family systems theory views two other systems as important and related to the concept of the emotional system. These are the feeling and intellectual systems.

Transferences are to psychoanalytic theory and practice as emotional fusion is to Bowen family systems theory. Emotional fusion is used in family systems theory as the equivalent to the concept of transference.

During Bowen's training in psychoanalytic theory and practice, he was immersed in the world of transferences and countertransferences, as were other early family therapists. However, in his NIMH project, he began to think differently about these concepts. While recognizing their powerful influences, Bowen wondered about the possibility of reducing the intensity of transferences with the project families. Was this possible? How could it be accomplished?

Viewing the family as an emotional unit and recognizing how challenging it was to work with the families on an inpatient unit, a new clinical direction emerged. The last three years were then spent working with the families in a daily staff–family meeting. The results of these meetings were twofold; the groups were successful in better managing the emotions within each family, and they assisted staff in managing their overinvolvements with the family members. Bowen (2013) commented that the staff who did the best at managing their overinvolvements had the best control over their countertransference reactions.

Today the concepts of transference and countertransference remain in family systems theory, but the conceptual basis has changed. There remains an emphasis on coaching therapists to better manage their emotional reactions by learning theory, ongoing supervision, and working on basic differentiation of self.

Kerr. In his classic book, *Family Evaluation*, Kerr has comments about the concept of transference (Kerr & Bowen, 1988). For example, he notes that the role of the therapist based on family systems theory guides the therapist to have contact with the clinical problems but not get emotionally overinvolved with them. This is the concept of emotional detachment or emotional neutrality. In this way, "this type of contact can reduce symptoms but without replicating the patient's unresolved emotional attachments" (Kerr & Bowen, 1988, p. 110). Kerr also thinks that the therapist can be helpful to the patient or patients without intensifying transferences.

In a nod to the importance of theory, Kerr explicates a basic difference between how psychoanalytic theory and Bowen family systems theory view the concept of transference. Family systems views transference as one type of emotional fusion. He goes on to note the conceptual differences between a family systems and psychoanalytic view of transferences. For example, in psychoanalytic theory the concept of transference/countertransference is forever associated with the concept of the unconscious. On the other hand, in family systems theory, emotional fusion is theoretically linked to the concept of the emotional system (Kerr & Bowen, 1988). Further trying to distinguish the emotional system from the unconscious, Kerr notes that the concepts of transference and countertransference outline therapist–patient behavioral interactions. With family systems theory, the concept of triangles highlights the emotional and verbal interactions in a family system of two or more people.

Kerr outlines and highlights the importance of the family systems concept of differentiation of self, which is roughly equivalent to emotional maturity (Kerr & Bowen, 1988). Our parents are viewed "as the original transference relationship" and that working to change oneself while in contact to past and present family relationships is "the highroad to increasing basic level of self" (Kerr & Bowen, 1988, p. 276).

East. Chris East, PsyD, is both a Presbyterian minister and a psychologist who works at Replacements, Inc., as a consultant. East has participated in several years of the postgraduate program at the Bowen Center for the Study of the Family and, following this, has participated in research seminars at the Bowen Center and now at the Bowen Theory Academy.

East has a longstanding interest in the concept of transference in both psychoanalytic psychotherapy and Bowen family systems theory and practice. In an unpublished paper presented to a research seminar, East distinguished Bowen's and Freudian approaches to this important concept. He concluded, "where Bowen differed from Freud is not the reality of the transference nor the need to resolve the transference, but in the therapeutic stance the therapist adopts vis-a-vis the transference" (2008, p. 3). Rather than Freud's emphasis on insight, "Bowen offered the alternative view that it is the therapist's own *maturity* which is the critical component in psychotherapy" (p. 4). It was the ability of the therapist to address his/her own differentiation of self that is critical.

THE REAL RELATIONSHIP

Traditional Perspectives

Gelso. Gelso and collaborators viewed the real relationship as "the personal relationship between therapist and patient marked by the extent to which each is genuine with the other and perceives/experiences the other in ways that benefit the other" (Gelso, 2014, p. 119).

Meissner. According to Meissner, "the real relation involves those other aspects of interaction between the psychoanalyst or therapist and patient that reflect their existence and status as real persons functioning in the real world" (p. 265).

Family Systems Perspectives

Of the three components of the therapeutic relationship, it is the real relationship component that most distinguishes Gelso's and Meissner's approaches from family systems theory and practice. On a basic level, Gelso's and Meissner's orientation is primarily on the therapist–patient dyad, whereas family systems clinicians have a primary focus on work outside the consulting room with the patient and their significant emotional relationships. The therapist–patient relationships in the room are considered of secondary interest. The two people who have most contributed to this perspective in family systems theory in this area will be reviewed.

Bowen. Bowen's interest in the real relationship formally began in the mid-1950s, although he never used this term. This date corresponds with his family project at NIMH. His interest was both theoretical and clinical. It was theoretical in the guiding principle of the family as an emotional unit. This principle signaled a shift from a person in the family with symptoms to the nuclear family with a person who has problems. The focus on the patient's family replaced the traditional therapist–patient dyad in importance. The clinical direction also changed to the patient's family as an emotional resource and a crucible for emotional reactivity. The therapist took an outside role. Bowen's work with the project families was his first documented effort to highlight efforts to help young adults address unresolved issues with their parents and to help parents to separate emotionally from their children.

One of Bowen's chief goals was to work with family members to increase their basic level of differentiation. Often this was in a family member, generally the family leader. The reader should note that he described two kinds of differentiation—basic and functional. Basic differentiation is established with people when they leave home but can be increased with ongoing efforts. Functional differentiation is negotiated or borrowed in relationships with significant others. Differences in these variables are reflected in the variety of life courses people can have within multigenerational families (Bowen, 1978).

Bowen's concept of emotional cutoff was added to his theory in 1975. This concept described how people managed their emotionality with their parents or the adults who raised them. Bowen (1978) provided details about the concept by stating that people manage emotional cutoff by various internal means or by physical distance.

Bowen's seminal contribution during his time at the Georgetown Family Center (now the Bowen Center for the Study of the Family) is that a motivated person with a coach can detour around problems in their marriage or nuclear family to resolve issues with their parents. Bowen noted that people who undertake such a journey often find that their presenting problem in the marriage or family resolves.

Last, Bowen believed, taught, and wrote that the real relationship is not something that is just for family members; he thought that the therapist must address his/her own unresolved matters with his/her nuclear family. About this topic, he wrote:

> I believe and teach that the therapist usually has the very same problems in his own family that are present in families he sees professionally, and that he has a responsibility to define himself in his own family if he is to function adequately in his own work. (Bowen, 1978, p. 468)

Kerr. Kerr's work built on the work of Bowen in the area of the importance of the patient's family in their treatment. Specifically, Kerr (1988) stresses the goal of increasing the basic level of differentiation of the patient or patients. It is one's basic level of differentiation that is dependent on the degree of emotional separation the person achieves when leaving home. Emotional cutoff using physical or emotional distance is the concept in family systems theory describing how individuals manage their unresolved attachments to their parents. There is great variation in the degree of emotional separation people have when leaving their family of origin, and this results in differing levels of basic differentiation. "Complete differentiation exists in a person who has fully resolved the emotional attachment to his family" (Kerr & Bowen, 1988, p. 97).

Changing one's basic level of differentiation is best done in relationships to emotionally significant others, meaning primarily one's family. Noting the importance of having an action plan to resolve these emotional problems, Kerr (1978) concludes:

> Thirty years of clinical experience with therapy based on family systems theory very strongly suggests that the most productive approach for increasing basic level of differentiation is family psychotherapy with a person who is motivated to bridge the emotional cutoff from his family of origin. (p. 286)

In the final chapter, I will compare the distinctive features of psychodynamic psychotherapy and cognitive-behavioral therapy with family psychotherapy/coaching.

Part Four

Chapter Eight

The Distinctive Features of Family Psychotherapy and Coaching in Bowen Family Systems Theory

DISTINCTIVE FEATURES OF FAMILY PSYCHOTHERAPY AND COACHING

> There is always some kind of therapeutic involvement, but the question is what kind of involvement? (Meissner, 2000, p. 513)

The interest in the distinctive features in psychotherapy first came to me while reviewing a 2010 article on *The Efficacy of Psychodynamic Psychotherapy* by Jonathan Shedler. Although the main focus of his article was on the empirical evidence for the efficacy of psychodynamic therapy, the first section highlighted the distinctive features of psychodynamic psychotherapy.

Shedler (2010) offered a concise definition of treatment based on psychodynamic psychotherapy:

> The essence of psychodynamic therapy is exploring those aspects of self that are not fully known, especially as they are manifested and potentially influenced in the therapy relationship. (p. 98)

Shedler (2010) also reviews several research studies defining psychodynamic psychotherapy and helps to distinguish it from other psychotherapies. He based his analysis on Blagys and Hilsenroth (2000, 2002), who examined the comparative psychotherapy process literature on psychodynamic-interpersonal and cognitive-behavioral psychotherapy.

Hilsenroth and Blagys (2002) summarize their work on the psychometric development of the Comparative Psychotherapy Process Scale (CPPS). The CPPS was designed to evaluate the distinctive features of cognitive-behavioral and psychodynamic therapies. The results were from an examination of video recordings of clinical sessions rather than a survey of clinicians.

The goals of this chapter include: first, a review of the distinctive features of psychodynamic-interpersonal and cognitive-behavioral therapies based on the work of Hilsenroth and Blagys (2002). Second, the distinctive features of family psychotherapy, based on Bowen family systems theory, are reviewed in two areas: conceptual frameworks and therapist behaviors. This is not the first effort to examine components of psychotherapy based on Bowen family systems theory. For example, Gilbert (2008), in a presentation at the postgraduate program at the Bowen Center for the Study of the Family, outlined nine features of psychotherapy based on Bowen family systems theory. Recently, Kerr (2013) wrote of seven core ideas of Bowen theory's concepts of human emotional functioning and how these concepts inform the psychotherapy process. A third goal is to begin to operationalize the role of the family psychotherapist using Bowen family systems theory. Just what therapist behaviors consistently appear in clinical sessions? How do these differ from other methods of psychotherapy?

DISTINCTIVE FEATURES OF PSYCHODYNAMIC PSYCHOTHERAPY

Blagys and Hilsenroth (2000) identified seven therapeutic activities that "consistently and significantly" distinguish psychodynamic psychotherapy from cognitive-behavioral treatment (Hilsenroth et al. 2002, p. 341). These seven areas of psychoanalytic psychotherapy include: (a) focusing on expression of emotion and affect, (b) exploring efforts by patients to avoid problem feelings and thoughts, (c) recognizing recurrent pattern and themes, (d) discussing past experiences with significant family members, (e) highlighting important interpersonal relationships, (f) attending to the therapeutic relationship, and (g) assessing the patient's fantasies.

DISTINCTIVE FEATURES OF COGNITIVE-BEHAVIORAL THERAPY

Hilsenroth et al. (2002) derived six therapeutic activities that distinguished cognitive-behavioral therapy from psychodynamic treatment: (a) assigning out-of-session homework, (b) being active in the direction of session activities, (c) the teaching of coping skills, (d) focusing on the future experiences of patients, (e) giving information to patients concerning their therapy and diagnosis or diagnoses, and (f) attending to the patient's fantasies.

CONCISE DEFINITION OF FAMILY PSYCHOTHERAPY

Following Shedler's (2010) brief definition of psychoanalytic psychotherapy, a concise definition of family psychotherapy is proposed: Family psychotherapy/coaching means knowing family systems theory and focusing on enhancing the differentiation of self of both the therapist and family members. Clinical practice guidelines follow from this definition.

DISTINCTIVE FEATURES OF FAMILY PSYCHOTHERAPY/COACHING

Foundations

Primary emphasis on theory. Bowen would certainly agree with Gelso and Hayes (1998) that the "psychotherapists theoretical orientation is deeply connected to their theory of the psychotherapy relationship" (Gelso & Hayes, 1998, p. 15). This is especially true with family psychotherapy based on Bowen theory. A long-term study and application of the concepts of Bowen theory to the therapist's own family and their clinical cases is more important than techniques. To facilitate the study of theory, it is suggested that the therapist become involved in some type of formal postgraduate program modeled after the Bowen Center for the Study of the Family. There are many such programs throughout the United States. Ongoing work with a coach/supervisor in the application of theoretical concepts to the therapist's own family, clinical cases, or work situations is a part of all of these programs. Family psychotherapy is a theoretical-therapeutic system where therapy follows from theory (Kerr & Bowen, 1988).

Bowen theory is a "theoretical-therapeutic system in which theory determines therapy, and observations from therapy can in turn modify the theory" (Bowen, 1978, p. 156). There is an interaction in family psychotherapy between theory and therapy. This is a position that continues from Bowen's early work with families at NIMH. By knowing, studying, and applying theory to the important relationships of the therapist, their clinical situations are more manageable.

The concept of the emotional system. The unconscious is to psychoanalysis as the emotional system is to Bowen theory. This is a central concept in family systems theory. Bowen used this concept to replace the idea of an unconscious in Freudian theory (Bowen, 1978; Kerr & Bowen, 1988). Specifically, Bowen (1978) concluded that the concept "obviates the use of the unconscious to postulate a cause" (p. 189). Furthermore, Kerr (1988) determined

that it was also unnecessary "to invoke a concept of 'unconscious motiva-
tion'" to account for the behaviors of family units (p. 5). The emotional system includes both the feeling and intellectual systems. The emotional system
is defined as the "behavior of all forms of life is driven and regulated by the
same life forces" (Kerr & Bowen, 1988, p. 28). "The term *emotional* refers
to the force that motivates the system and the 'relationship' to the ways it
is expressed" (Bowen, 1978, p. 158). The concept of the emotional systems
relates people to all living things.

Family systems concepts. The concepts of nuclear family emotional processes and family project processes were mentioned in early papers; these
parts of family systems theory developed over a six-year period, between
1957 and 1963 (Bowen, 1978, p. 357). "The notion that all human problems
exist on a single continuum gave rise by the early 1960s, to the concept of differentiation of self" (Bowen, 1978, p. 358). The concept of triangles, another
of the basic concepts in the theory, began in 1957 when it was termed the
independent triad (Bowen, 1978, p. 358). The multigenerational transmission
process concept was started in 1955 and was fully developed in about 1960
at the end of the Family Study Project. Sibling position was added based on
Toman's *Family Constellation* (Toman, 1961). Emotional cutoff was included
as a concept in Bowen theory in 1975, and in that year, family systems theory
changed its name to Bowen theory (Bowen, 1978, p. 358). Clinical practice
rests on a foundation of these theoretical concepts. The therapist must know
and study these concepts.

Differentiation of self—a cornerstone concept. Many authors writing
about family systems theory comment that differentiation of self is a key
concept in family systems theory (see Bowen, 1978; Kerr & Bowen, 1988);
however, the concept is complex, and a challenge to initially understand and
operationalize. A sustained effort is needed to personally address this concept.
Differentiation of self is said to exist on a continuum (low-medium-high) but
is not represented in a normal statistical distribution. That is, Bowen thought
few if any people were in the top quartile of this variable (Bowen, 1978; Kerr
& Bowen, 1988). It is unknown how basic differentiation is distributed in
the population. Bowen's scale of differentiation was primarily designed to
obtain a theoretical understanding rather than to be used as a psychometric
instrument. In addition, there are two aspects of differentiation—basic and
functional. It is basic differentiation that is established when the person leaves
home; functional differentiation describes the interchange of self in family
relationships. Increasing a family member's basic level of differentiation is
the main goal of family psychotherapy and coaching. Attention to differentiation of self is important for the therapist and his/her patients in clinical
practice.

In terms of methods to increase differentiation, Kerr (2015)[3] suggests the following:

> One tried and true pathway: serious engagement with Bowen theory; objectivity about the emotional processes in one's own life; consequent emotional neutrality: beyond blame; action for self that does not disrupt relationships; and repeating this many times in important relationships.

In Kerr and Bowen's (1988) words, "increasing one's ability to distinguish between thinking and feeling within self and others and learning to use that ability to direct one's life and solve problems is the central guiding principle of family psychotherapy" (p. 98).

The structure of the consultation can facilitate this principle. For example, anything that can be done to enhance thinking and reduce emotionality is helpful. A previous example was given by structuring a marital session by having each person of the dyad interact with the therapist while the other person observes. Differentiation of self is not a one-way street; having therapists engage in a long-term effort to work on their own differentiation of self is useful. The search for and nurturing of a family leader is an effort to increase that person's level of differentiation of self. In fact, Bowen (2013) observed that it was the family leaders who first undertook this work.

The family as an emotional unit—another cornerstone concept. Another cornerstone of family systems theory is the concept of the family as an emotional unit. This was the primary finding of Bowen's Family Study Project. After reviewing Bowen's original papers recently published in an edited book, my question is, what prompted Bowen's shift away from a traditional view of the therapeutic relationship (Bowen, 2013)? The reader will recall that he was first trained as a psychoanalyst at the Menninger Clinic. My reading of his early papers from the NIMH project and later writings in his 1978 book is that his shift away from conventional practice was primarily due to the concept of the family as an emotional unit. His experiences during the NIMH project working with family units provided the unique opportunity to see families 24/7 in action with one member having severe emotional problems. He saw much more than a person with serious symptoms in a family; he witnessed emotional interdependence in families. In his book *Family Therapy in Clinical Practice* (1978), a section of a chapter was entitled "The Therapeutic Relationship in a Broader Perspective" (p. 342). This broad perspective is possible with the concept of the family as an emotional unit.

Both Meissen's and Gelso's tripartite view of the therapeutic relationship brings to mind a basic question: What are the components of the therapeutic relationship in family psychotherapy and coaching? Does the tripartite model have applicability to the therapeutic role in family systems theory? It was Meissner's extensive writings on the various aspects of the therapeutic relationship that focused thinking about the specific components within in family psychotherapy/coaching as Bowen described this process. In his writings during and after the NIMH Family Study Project, Bowen was careful to distinguish his view of a relationship from a traditional view of the therapeutic–patient relationship. He thought that family psychotherapy coaching entailed a significantly different therapeutic process compared to therapeutic relationships in psychoanalytic psychotherapy and family therapy. This is because the therapist has a different role and this position in family systems theory is nested within the concept of the family as an emotional unit (see Bowen, 2013).

The concept of the family as a unit also guides family assessment. At least three generations of the family are evaluated in terms of their overall functioning. The concept of the family as an emotional unit applies regardless of who is in the consulting room—individuals, couples, or families.

Interface with the accepted sciences. A distinguishing characteristic of family systems theory is its long history in working to establish connections to the social and physical sciences. In fact, past Symposiums on Family Theory & Family Psychotherapy, held annually in November, often feature guest lecturers from outside traditional mental health disciplines.

In the beginning Bowen cast his concepts in biological terms. He made a sustained effort to move toward the accepted sciences with his theory. He wrote, "the scientific facts of evolution have been chosen to replace many of the ideas in Freudian theory" (Kerr & Bowen, 1988). He aligned his theory within the principles of evolution and viewed the human as a product of evolutionary processes.

An example of the emphasis on establishing and continuing a relationship with the sciences is a recent edited book using the family emotional system as an integrated concept for clinical practice, science, and systems theory (Noone & Papero, 2015). The reader will recall that the concept of the family as an emotional unit was the main finding of Bowen's NIMH Family Study Project. A survey of the chapters of this book reveals contributions from family systems theorists, clinicians, and scientists relating the concept to nonhuman primates, social wasps, and ants. The family as an emotional unit concept also influences research and clinical practice.

Relationship to evolutionary theory. The concepts of Bowen family systems theory were developed based on the perspective that apart from some unique features, humans (*homo sapiens*) are the result of evolutionary processes. The clinician would have to be open to this perspective. This openness would include reading in this area and attending conference presentations about evolutionary processes and how humans relate to other species. As Bowen concluded, "Evolution contradicts the notion that family relationships were developed by the human family" (Bowen, 1987, p. 1). Reading other related literature is useful. For example, triangles or triadic relationships are important in human relationships. It seems they are important in chimpanzee families as well (deWaal & Embree, 1997). The goal is to obtain a broad perspective of human functioning; other species can teach us a lot about human relationships.

The emergence of a new perspective on human development. Before and early in the project, there was the focus on symbiosis within the mother–daughter dyads and theories about maternal inadequacy. During the last three years of the project, Bowen came to recognize the unresolved mother–child symbiosis as an "arrest" of normal development and that psychotic symptoms were "superimposed" on these (Bowen, 1995, p. 31). Bowen also believed there was a continuum of unresolved symbiotic attachments from the least to the most intense (Bowen, 1995, p. 32). It is not too little attachment that Bowen saw as problematic but overattachment (Bowen, 1995, p. 27). This represented a very different view of attachment from that pioneered by John Bowlby. For a historical comparison, Bowlby's three landmark presentations to the British Psychoanalytic Society in London, on the child's ties to their mothers, separation anxiety, and grief were published near the end or after the completion of Bowen's project (Bretherton, 1992). Both Bowen and Bowlby addressed the concept of attachment about the same time, but each had a different focus; Bowlby emphasized mother–child dyads, and Bowen studied families.

Family diagrams. Family diagrams first originated in the Family Study Project. Known today by some as genograms, the term was proposed by Phil Guerin, one of Bowen's students (Butler, 2008). Family diagrams are a means of graphically displaying factual information about multigenerational families. In this case, a picture is indeed worth a thousand words. The factual information recorded on family diagrams reflects emotional processes across families.

While the symbols for family diagrams are not standardized, some basic symbols have been suggested. An early example is a one-page guide, *Key to the Use of the Genogram (Family Diagram)* by Bowen (1980). In this one page Bowen (1980) suggested the key elements that family diagrams should include as well as a key to basic symbols. Kerr and Bowen (1988), in a chapter on family evaluation, also suggest basic symbols for use in family diagrams. The use of family diagrams is a standard aspect of consultations in clinical practice based on family systems theory. A whiteboard or blackboard is a useful addition in many offices of family psychotherapists and coaches. This medium is very useful in drawing family diagrams or illustrating emotional processes in families.

IMPORTANT THERAPIST PERSPECTIVES

Working to establish viable emotional contact. Meissner's (1996a) article on empathy stimulated my thinking about one of Bowen's comments. That is, Bowen believed viable emotional contact between the therapist and family, couples, or family members was essential in clinical work. Bowen also mentions another type of emotional contact. That is, the quality and frequency of contacts (e.g., calling, texting, or visiting) between adult children and their parents. In family systems theory regular emotional contact is the opposite of emotional cutoff, that is, having no contact of any type with one's parents. My thinking, however, focused on the term *viable emotional contact* that Bowen wrote and spoke about. I wondered whether this was equated with the empathy that Meissner thought was important.

On the subject of empathy, however, Bowen (1978) was clear when he said, "I don't know about the empathy things—I don't deal too much in empathy" (p. 525). In his NIMH Family Study Project, the average length of stay was about a year. Families would not remain in an inpatient setting this long without having some emotional connections to the project and staff. In addition, when one sees clinical interviews of Bowen, his interest and respect is clearly present. People viewing his tapes might conclude he was being empathetic. But, in family systems theory, empathy is not the same as viable emotional contact.

Viable emotional contact is a term used in family systems theory writings and discussions but is never clearly defined. Thanks to ebooks and their search function, it is easy to determine the number of times these terms are used in Bowen's (1978) book and Kerr and Bowen's (1982) text and whether there is a clarification. This term is used many times in both sources but is not defined. It is important to have emotional contact between the therapist and family members, so in my view viable contact refers to some degree of emotional connection between the therapist and a family as a whole or family member. In addition to viable emotional contact, family systems theory adds an important dimension of having the therapist self-monitor his/her own emotional involvement. The risks of emotional overinvolvement and how to manage this using differentiation of self is an important contribution of Bowen family systems theory.

Michael Kerr, MD, recalls comments attributed to Dr. Bowen on this issue of viable emotional contact in clinical consultations with families:

> I don't know how Dr. Bowen would define emotional contact. I first heard him use the phrase in the 1980s, I think after watching Phil Guerin interview a family. Dr. Bowen, said, as I recall, "Phil made solid emotional contact with every member of that family." Another comment he made about a clinical family he had recently seen was "at the end of the session, the wife said that I was a caring

person. I didn't say it, but I thought, I would say that I am interested in the problems and you interpret that as caring." My way of interpreting emotional contact is the family members leave a session thinking that you have listened, take an interest in them and their problems, and have some understanding of their difficulties. This depends some on being able to imagine what the other is feeling, but also on theory and emotional objectivity. Viable implies to me that the family members . . . that they could be helped in such an environment. (M. E Kerr, personal communication, June 9, 2014)

Neutrality in clinical practice. Meissner (1998) wrote in detail about the concept of emotional neutrality. His article on neutrality and the alliance focused on the therapist's ability to be continually aware and manage their countertransference reactions in clinical situations. In his NIMH papers, Bowen stated that the staff members who could best master their counter-transference reactions were better able to function more effectively with the project families (Bowen, 2013).

According to Meissner, neutrality has long been considered as important in psychoanalytic psychotherapy. And in his early papers, Bowen agreed. Moving from the traditional therapist–patient therapeutic relationship to family psychotherapy, Bowen applied this concept to the family as a unit (Bowen, 2013). Figuratively, it was as if the family instead of an individual patient were on the couch. Bowen sought as much neutrality as possible about the interactions in the family unit and termed it *emotional nonparticipation.* Today this term is known as *emotional neutrality.*

Several of Bowen's important original papers on the Family Study Project were published after his death (Bowen, 2013). The term *neutrality* is not used in these early papers but the phrase *emotional detachment* is discussed. For example, Bowen (2013) noted that working to achieve awareness of the family means monitoring and reducing overinvolvement with individuals in the family. Overinvolvement with any family member compromises efforts to maintain emotional detachment or neutrality.

In Bowen's classic book, *Family Therapy in Clinical Practice* (1978), he describes and defines emotional nonparticipation/emotional neutrality:

> Emotional nonparticipation or staying out of the family emotional system does not mean the therapist is cold, distant and aloof. Instead, it requires the therapist to recognize his own emotional involvement when it does occur, to gain suffi-cient control over his emotional system to avoid emotional side-taking with any family member, to observe the family as a phenomenon and to be able to relate freely to any family member at any time. (p. 191)

In Kerr and Bowen's classic 1988 book, *Family Evaluation*, detachment and emotional neutrality are linked. Kerr viewed it as a therapeutic ability to remain in contact with a clinical problem but not become overinvolved with the problem. "Neutrality is reflected as an ability to be calm about what goes on between others, to be aware of all the emotionality sides of an issue, and to be aware of the influence of subjectivity on one's notions about what 'should' be" (Kerr & Bowen, 1988, p. 111). While Kerr (1988) thinks that complete emotional neutrality is impossible to achieve, this ability can be increased by a careful and long-term work by the therapist on his/her self and his/her own family. "Neutrality becomes differentiation when it is operationalized through one's actions in a relationship" (Kerr & Bowen, 1988, p. 111).

Psychologically replacing parents. While psychologically replacing parents during psychotherapy was standard clinical practice at the time, Bowen proposed an alternative. He concluded:

> One point would be that the therapist might develop techniques in which he did not lend himself to the patient's bid that he do a certain amount of "replacing of the parent." Experience would indicate that the patients do in fact need such a figure. If this be so, then who should this figure be? (Bowen, 2013, p. 47)

What was the basis for this conclusion? If not the therapist, then who? Based on theory and clinical experiences with project families, Bowen determined that the *figure* should be the patient's family rather than the therapist. This of course partly stemmed from the project's theoretical focus on the family as an emotional unit. In addition, Bowen concluded that the emotionality normally managed within the therapeutic relationship should be placed within the family. Handling the intense daily emotionality by working with the project families presented significant challenges for the staff (Bowen, 2013). In summary, there were both theoretical and clinical reasons for adopting this alternative therapeutic position.

Psychologically replacing a parent in psychotherapy, especially with minor children, is alive and well today, but has received little attention in terms of potential risks. For example, one risk in separating children from their parent(s) is that once in therapy, the family's anxiety decreases but the family projection to the child increases. In addition, after writing about this concept in his unpublished papers, Bowen never again wrote about this subject.

The therapist declines to take on the role of psychologically replacing parents. Instead, the parents are assisted to coach their child. Seeing family as a unit is one step toward the implementation of this rule. If the therapist works to not psychologically replace a parent, then a void exists. Who fills this void? The answer is a family leader, which is a job held by a person inside the family. In fact, during the project, Bowen expected the family leaders to begin family sessions, while he observed and commented about family processes.

The therapist works to minimize psychologically replacing parents or guardians. In practice, however, the role is challenging to undertake. Parents are often in a helpless position with a child and seek *expert* assistance. Bowen's term for this was *emotional nonparticipation.* This means that the therapist diligently works to manage his/her own emotional reactivity and avoid overinvolvement. In fact, Bowen commented that the staff who could best manage their overinvolvement also had the best control over their countertransference reactions (Bowen, 2013). One method used during the Family Study Project was to see the entire family unit and decline attempts for individual relationships. Even in cases where the family leader presented alone, the focus remained on the family unit (Bowen, 2013). It is quite common for parents to bring their child for evaluation or treatment for *someone to talk to*, which is a plea for expert assistance. While this position can be avoided, the therapist can tell parents that the therapist will coach them so that they can coach their own child.

Meissner's (1999) comments about the parental model directed my thinking to Bowen's (2013) cautions about psychologically replacing parents in psychotherapy. It seems almost second nature with parents that if there are emotional problems with their child, they take the child for evaluation and/or treatment not themselves. It is atypical for a parent(s) to come to psychotherapy without their child saying they or the family play some part in the child's problems.

Bowen cautioned about psychologically replacing parents in psychotherapy and suggested that the coach work with parents to be more effective with their own children. Basamania (2013) relates that with family psychotherapy, as opposed to individual psychotherapy, the family is kept intact. A helpless position for parents is indicated by the oft heard refrain "he/she needs someone to talk to." The participation of children in family psychotherapy is conceptualized and practiced differently in family psychotherapy than in individual or family therapy. For example, family psychotherapy when possible includes children and their parents. This was the central treatment plan within the Family Study Project. On an outpatient basis during and after Bowen's project, there were ongoing efforts to move the problem back to the parents and slowly remove children from psychotherapy. The family psychotherapist works to replace the child in the triangle with the parents. There are instances, however, where individual sessions with children are unavoidable. For example, Bowen (1978) did work with parents and children alone to help them emotionally separate from each other. But the central focus remains primarily on the adult caretakers of children rather than on individual or play therapy with children that excludes their adult caretakers.

Often the child is in individual psychotherapy or play therapy and the parents or the family is referred for conjoint or family therapy, respectively. Bowen commented about this complication as follows:

> I conceive of a transference relationship as an emotional sub-system which, in too many cases, serves to stabilize the emotional system of the family without getting at the basic issue between the parents. (Bowen, 2015, p. 52)

Maturity and immaturity. Bowen has an interesting notion about the concepts of maturity and immaturity in both patients and therapists. Bowen's view of this process from immaturity to maturity, not involving psychoanalytic theory, was outlined in his early papers; he concludes that both the patient and therapist have mature and immature sides (Bowen, 2013). He illustrated this with a circle divided in half, one half for the mature side and the other for the immature side. Bowen concluded that the goal of family psychotherapy was to have the therapist's mature side relate to the mature side of the patient rather than their immature side. Another goal was to have the patient's mature side manage their own immature side rather than using the therapist–patient relationship. Bowen's (2013) perspective is different from the psychoanalytic and the view elaborated by Gelso et al. (2008).

Triangles. The concept of triangles is unique to family systems theory and practice. It is one of Bowen's eight interlocking concepts in his theory. This concept describes how a triangle is the basic building block in a family rather than a dyad. Not only are triangles important in families, they are also important in clinical practice.

The therapist is part of triangle in many situations: with two parents without their children, in a couple, and with a family as a whole. Within a family there are several triangles possible. A fundamental rule with triangles in clinical practice is that if the therapist can take a neutral position and relate to both parties calmly, the other two people will calm down and the level of anxiety will automatically decrease (Bowen, 1978). It is the position taken by the therapist that is most important rather than what is said. Perfection is not required; the therapist only has to be calmer than two other people. Triangles are universal in families, work situations, and clinical practice. Clinical practice becomes a study of triangles and management of the emotionality that arises from them.

Transferences and countertransferences. These two concepts have been retained in family systems theory and practice; however, the conceptual basis has shifted from the concept of the unconscious to the concept of the emotional system. Clinicians use family systems theory as a basis for practice and personal work with their family, to respect the emotionality inherent in clinical work and endeavor to use differentiation of self as a remedy to reduce the impact of emotionality. Automatic reactivity, as noted by Gilbert (1992), is always present in both clinical and ongoing work with one's family. It is actually present in all relationships.

In an article about the original Family Study Project, Basamania (Bowen, 2013) noted the diluting effect of working with family units on both transferences and countertransferences. Bowen demonstrated during the Family Study Project that it was possible to achieve behavioral and emotional changes within individuals and families without interpreting transferences. This finding is another important contribution of this project.

Family leadership. This section on family leadership is a logical extension of the previous one on avoiding psychologically replacing parents. If the therapist does not assume the role of psychologically replacing parents, then who does? Bowen's answer was that it should be the patient's family and, therefore, the focus should be on seeing that a family leader emerged.

Family members always seem to know the name of the family leader. In clinical work it is important that the family leader be identified. Initially, the leader was in a helpless position with some degree of paralysis. In addition, it was the family leader who first began to work on his/her own differentiation (Bowen, 2013). The concept of family leadership is an important one in family psychotherapy but has received little attention in Bowen family system theory.

It was important to identify the family leader within each family on the unit. Once the family leader was identified, it became important to help this person become a more effective leader. If he/she is helpless, then exploring how he/she can become less helpless is important.

In the Family Study Project, the family leader was requested to begin sessions and told that therapist would intervene only when the leader was at an impasse. Family leaders were also requested to summarize the session. With the outpatient families, the leader was also responsible for setting up follow-up appointments.

The initial technique is of course to locate a family leader. Once identified, the family leader is often in a helpless state and passive position. In that position, the therapist is expected to provide guidance, direction, and answers. The invitation, however, must be politely declined. Otherwise, the adults in the family will sit back and wait for the therapist.

Teaching the functioning of emotional systems. Teaching family members about how emotional systems operate in families can be illustrated in clinical sessions. Besides a session summary that is requested of family leaders, it is a useful clinical activity to highlight which family systems concepts might apply to the problem.

SUMMARY

Bowen's work in the Family Study Project introduced an alternative model of the traditional therapeutic relationship. This change had both a theoretical and clinical basis. The theoretical part was the concept of the family as an emotional unit. If the family is conceptualized as an emotional unit with a person with symptoms, then the attention must be on that family unit. This concept guides both assessment and treatment. The clinical basis involved how the intense emotionality is managed between a family and therapist. Bowen also departed from his own training by advocating leaving the emotionality in the family rather than placing and interpreting this in the context of the therapeutic dyad. He also recommended the therapist monitor their overinvolvement with any one family member. Family psychotherapy was and remains a very different way to work clinically with people. Bowen's work points to moving past the therapist–patient dyad to the family as an emotional unit. In addition, family systems theory uses different terms to describe clinical processes. For example, *automatic reactivity* replaces the term *transference* because that term is closely associated with psychoanalytic theory.

Notes

1. From "Family Psychotherapy: The First Evolutionary Stage During the NIMH Family Study Project," by John F. Butler, 2013, *Family Systems*, 10, 1, pp. 29–42. Used by permission.

2. From "Bowen's NIMH Family Study Project and the Origins of Family Psychotherapy," by John F. Butler, 2011, *Family Systems*, 8, 2, pp. 135–142. Used by permission.

3. "The Differentiation-Togetherness Concept of Counterbalancing Life Forces." PowerPoint presentation by Michael E. Kerr, MD, at Bowen Theory Academy, July 3, 2015. Used by permission.

References

Blagys, M. D., & Hilsenroth, M. J. (2000). Distinctive features of short-term psychodynamic-interpersonal psychotherapy: A review of the comparative psychotherapy process literature. *Clinical Psychology: Science and Practice*, 7, 167–188.

Blagys, M. D., & Hilsenroth, M. J. (2002). Distinctive features of short-term cognitive-behavioral psychotherapy: A review of the comparative psychotherapy process literature. *Clinical Psychology Review*, 22, 671–706.

Bordin, E. S. (1979). The generalizability of the psychoanalytic concept of the working alliance. *Psychotherapy: Theory, Research & Practice*, 16, 252–260.

Bowen, M. (1955). *3E Project.* (Available from L. Murray Bowen papers, Accession 2006—003, Box 4.) History of Medicine Division, National Library of Medicine, Washington, DC.

Bowen, M. (1956a). *A study of family relationships in schizophrenia and the therapeutic response when the family group is treated in a specific therapeutic setting.* (Available from L. Murray Bowen papers, Accession 2006—003, Box 4.) History of Medicine Division, National Library of Medicine, Washington, DC.

Bowen, M. (1956b). *Individual project report. Study and treatment of schizophrenia as a family problem.* (Available from L. Murray Bowen papers, Accession 2006—003, Box 3.) History of Medicine Division, National Library of Medicine, Washington, DC.

Bowen, M. (1957a). *Summary of the program of the family study section for the calendar year 1957.* (Available from L. Murray Bowen papers, Accession 2006—003, Box 4.) History of Medicine Division, National Library of Medicine, Washington, DC.

Bowen, M. (1957b). *Individual project report for calendar year 1957: Study and treatment of schizophrenia as a family problem.* (Available from L. Murray Bowen papers, Accession 2006—003, Box 4.) History of Medicine Division, National Library of Medicine, Washington, DC.

Bowen, M. (1957c). *Adult Psychiatry Branch Section on Ward 3-E.* (Available from L. Murray Bowen papers, Accession 2006—003, Box 4.) History of Medicine Division, National Library of Medicine, Washington, DC.

Bowen, M. (1957d). *The family project.* (Available from L. Murray Bowen papers, Accession 2006—003, Box 8.) History of Medicine Division, National Library of Medicine, Washington, DC.

Bowen, M. (1958a). *The therapeutic treatment of the family as a unit: First draft of paper for American Orthopsychiatry Meeting.* (Available from L. Murray Bowen papers, Accession 2006—003, Box 3.) History Medicine Division, National Library of Medicine, Washington, DC.

Bowen, M. (1958b). *The development of techniques of dealing with five family units and some patterns observed in the transaction of those families.* (Available from L. Murray Bowen papers, Accession 2006—003, Box 3.) History of Medicine Division, National Library of Medicine, Washington, DC.

Bowen, M. (1970). *From couch to coach.* Abstract of paper presented at the Annual Georgetown Family Symposium, Georgetown University, Washington, DC.

Bowen, M. (1978). *Family therapy in clinical practice.* Lanham, MD: Jason Aronson.

Bowen, M. (1980). Key in the use of the genogram (family diagram). In E. A. Carter & M. M. McGoldrick (Eds.), *The family life cycle: A framework for family therapy* (p. xxii). New York: Gardner Press.

Bowen, M. (1987). Psychotherapy, past, present, and future. In J. K. Zeig (Ed.), *The evolution of psychotherapy: The first conference* (pp. 32–44). New York: Brunner Mazel.

Bowen, M. (1995). A psychological formulation of schizophrenia. *Family Systems*, 2, 17–47.

Bowen, M. (2013). In J. F. Butler (Ed.), *The origins of family psychotherapy: The NIMH Family Study Project.* Lanham, MD: Jason Aronson.

Bowen, M. (2015). A letter from Murray Bowen to Dr. Alexander Gralick. *Family Systems*, 11, 49–60.

Bowen, M., Dysinger, R., Brodey, W., & Basamania, B. (1957). *The development of techniques of dealing with five family units and some patterns observed in the transaction of those families.* (Available from L. Murray Bowen papers, Accession 2006—003, Box 3.) History of Medicine Division, National Library of Medicine, Washington, DC.

Bretherton, I. (1992). The origins of attachment theory: John Bowlby and Mary Ainsworth. *Developmental Psychology*, 28, 759–775.

Butler, J. F. (2008). The family diagram and genogram: Comparisons and contrasts. *American Journal of Family Therapy*, 36, 169–180.

Castonguay, L. G., Constantino, M. J., & Holtforth, M. G. (2006). The working alliance: Where are we and where should we go? *Psychotherapy: Theory, Research, Practice, Training*, 43, 271–279.

Chertok, L. (1968). The discovery of the transference. *International Journal of Psychoanalysis*, 49, 560–576.

Cohen, J. (1988). *Statistical power analysis for the behavioral sciences* (2nd ed.) Hillsdale, NJ: Erlbaum.

Crits-Christoph, P., Gibbons, M. B. C., & Hearon, B. (2006). Does the alliance cause good outcome? Recommendations for future research on the alliance. *Psychotherapy: Theory, Research, Practice, Training*, 43, 280–285.

De Waal, F., & Embree, M. (1997). The triadic nature of primate social relationships. *Family Systems*, 4, 5–18.

East, C. (2008). *The place of transference: Freud and Bowen.* Presentation to Post-Graduate Research Seminar, Bowen Center for the Study of the Family, March 2008.

Fluckiger, C., Del Rey, A. C., Wampold, B. E., Symonds, D., & Horvath, A. O. (2012). How central is the alliance in psychotherapy? A multilevel longitudinal meta-analysis. *Journal of Counseling Psychology*, 59, 10–17.

Freud, S. (1912/1958). The dynamics of transference. In J. Strachey (Ed.), *The standard edition of the complete psychological work of Sigmund Freud* (Vol. 12, pp. 99–108). London, UK: Hogarth Press.

Friedlander, M. L., Escudero, V., & Heatherington, L. (2006). *The therapeutic alliance in couple and family therapy: An empirically informed guide to practice.* Washington, DC: American Psychological Association.

Friedlander, M. L., Escudero, V., Heatherington, L., & Diamond, G. M. (2011). Alliance in couple and family therapy. *Psychotherapy*, 48, 25–38.

Fuertes, J. N., Gelso, C. J., Owen, J., & Cheng, D. (2013). Real relationship, working alliance, transference/countertransference and outcome in time-limited counseling and psychotherapy. *Counseling Psychology Quarterly*, 26, 294–312.

Fuertes, J. N., Gelso, C. J., Owen, J., & Chang, D. (2015). Using the Inventory of Countertransference Behavior as an observer-rated measure. *Psychoanalytic Psychotherapy*, 29, 38–56.

Fuertes, J. N., Mislowack, A., Brown, S., Gur-Arsie, S., Wilkinson, S., & Gelso, C. J. (2007). Correlates of the real relationship in psychotherapy: A study of dyads. *Psychotherapy Research*, 17, 423–430.

Gelso, C. J. (2009). The real relationship in a postmodern world: Theoretical and empirical explorations. *Psychotherapy Research*, 19, 253–264.

Gelso, C. J. (2011). *The real relationship in psychotherapy: The hidden foundation of change.* Washington, DC: American Psychological Association.

Gelso, C. J. (2014). A tripartite model of the therapeutic relationship: Theory, research and practice. *Psychotherapy Research*, 24, 117–131.

Gelso, C. J., & Bhatia, A. (2012). Crossing theoretical lines: The role and effect of transference in nonanalytic psychotherapies. *Psychotherapy*, 49, 384–390.

Gelso, C. J., & Carter, J. A. (1985). The relationship in counseling and psychotherapy: Components, consequences, and theoretical antecedents. *The Counseling Psychologist*, 13, 155–243.

Gelso, J. C., & Carter, J. A. (1994). Components of the psychotherapy relationship: Their interaction and unfolding during treatment. *Journal of Counseling Psychology*, 41, 296–306.

Gelso, C. J., Fassinger, R. E., Gomez, M. J., & Latts, M. G. (1995). Countertransference reactions to lesbian clients: The role of homophobia, counselor gender, and countertransference management. *Journal of Counseling Psychology*, 42, 356–364.

Gelso, C. J., & Hayes, J. A. (1998). *The psychotherapy relationship: Theory, research, and practice.* New York: Wiley.

Gelso, C. J., & Hayes, J. A. (2001). Countertransference management. *Psychotherapy,* 38, 418–422.

Gelso, C. J., & Hayes, J. A. (2002). The management of countertransference. In J. C. Norcross (Ed.), *Therapeutic relationships that work* (pp. 267–283). New York: Oxford University Press.

Gelso, C. J., & Hayes, J. A. (2007). *Countertransference and the therapist's inner experience: Perils and possibilities.* Mahwah, NJ: Erlbaum.

Gelso, J. C., Hill, C. E., & Kivlighan, D. M. (1991). Transference, insight, and the counselor's intention during a counseling hour. *Journal of Counseling and Development,* 69, 428–433.

Gelso, C. J., Hill, C. E., Mohr, J. J., Rochlen, A. B., & Zack, J. (1999). Describing the face of transference: Psychodynamic therapists' recollections about transference in cases of successful long-term therapy. *Journal of Counseling Psychology,* 46, 257–267.

Gelso, C. J., Kelly, F. A., Fuertes, J. N., Marmarosh, C., Holmes, S., Costa, C., & Hancock, G. (2005). Measuring the real relationship in psychotherapy: Initial validation of the therapist form. *Journal of Counseling Psychology,* 52, 640–649.

Gelso, C. J., Kivlighan, D. M., Busa-Knepp, J., Spiegel, E. B., Ain, S., Hummel, A. M., & Markin, R. D. (2012). The unfolding of the real relationship and the outcome of brief psychotherapy. *Journal of Consulting Psychology,* 59, 395–406.

Gelso, C. J., Kivlighan, D. M., Wine, B., Jones, A., & Friedman, S. (1997). Transference, insight, and the course of time-limited psychotherapy. *Journal of Counseling Psychology,* 44, 209–217.

Gelso, C. J., Latts, M. G., Gomez, M. J., & Fassinger, R. E. (2002). Countertransference management and therapy outcome: An initial evaluation. *Journal of Clinical Psychology,* 58, 861–867.

Gelso, C. J., & Samstag, L. W. (2008). A tripartite model of the therapeutic relationship. In S. Brown & R. Lent (Eds.), *Handbook of counseling psychology* (4th ed., pp. 267–283). New York: Wiley.

Gelso, C. J., Williams, E. M., & Fretz, B. R. (2014). The therapeutic relationship. In *Counseling psychology* (3rd ed., pp. 217–248). Washington, DC: American Psychological Association.

Gilbert, R. M. (1992). *Extraordinary relationships.* Minneapolis, MN: Chromed Publishers.

Gilbert, R. M. (1999). *Connecting with our children.* New York: John Wiley.

Gilbert, R. M. (2004). *The eight concepts of Bowen theory.* Falls Church, VA: Leading Systems Press.

Gilbert, R. M. (2006). *Extraordinary leadership.* Falls Church, VA: Leading Systems Press.

Gilbert, R. M. (2008). *The cornerstone concept.* Falls Church, VA: Leading Systems Press.

Gilbert, R. M. (2011). Bowen family systems theory: The past, present, and the future. *Family Systems Forum,* 13, 6–8.

Greenson, R. R. (1965). The working alliance and the transference neurosis. *Psychoanalytic Quarterly*, 343, 155–181.

Greenson, R. R. (1967). *The technique and practice of psychoanalysis.* New York: International Universities Press.

Gullo, S., LoCoco, G., & Gelso, C. (2012). Early and later predicators of outcome in brief therapy: The role of the real relationship. *Journal of Clinical Psychology*, 68, 614–619.

Hargrove, D. S. (2009). Psychotherapy based on Bowen family systems theory. In J. H. Bray & M. Stanton (Eds.), *The Wiley-Blackwell handbook of family psychology.* Walden, MA: Wiley-Blackwell.

Harris, A. (2005). Transference, countertransference and the real relationship. In E. J. Person, A. M. Cooper, & G. Gabbard (Eds.), *Textbook of psychoanalysis* (pp. 201–216). Washington, DC: American Psychiatric Association Press

Hatcher, R. L., & Barends, A. W. (2006). How a return to theory could help alliance research? *Psychotherapy: Theory, Research, Practice, Training*, 43, 292–299.

Hayes, J., Gelso, C. J., & Hummel, A. M. (2011). Managing countertransference. *Psychotherapy*, 48, 88–97.

Hill, C. E. (2015). A festschrift for Charles Gelso. *Psychotherapy*, 52, 111–115.

Hilsenroth, M. J., Blagys, M. D., Ackerman, S. J., Bonge, R., & Blais, M. A. (2005). Measuring psychodynamic-interpersonal and cognitive-behavioral technique: Development of the comparative psychotherapy process scale. *Psychotherapy: Theory, Research, Practice, Training*, 42, 340–356.

Horvath, A. O. (2001). The alliance. *Psychotherapy, Theory, Research, Practice*, 38, 365–372.

Horvath, A. O. (2006). The alliance in context: Accomplishment, challenges, and future directions. *Psychotherapy: Theory, Research, Practice, Training*, 43, 258–263.

Horvath, A. O. (2013). You can't step into the same river twice, but you can stub your toes on the same rock: Psychotherapy outcome from a 50-year perspective. *Psychotherapy*, 50, 25–32.

Horvath, A. O., Fluckiger, A. C., & Symonds, D. C. (2011). Alliance in individual psychotherapy. *Psychotherapy*, 48, 25–33.

Horvath, A. O., & Greenburg, L. S. (1989). Development and validation of the working alliance inventory. *Journal of Counseling Psychology*, 36, 223–233.

Horvath, A. O., & Symonds, D. (1991). Relation between working alliance and outcome in psychotherapy: A meta-analysis. *Journal of Counseling Psychology*, 38, 139–149.

Kelley, F. A., Gelso, C. J., Fuertes, J. N., Marmarosh, C., & Lanier, S. (2010). The real relationship inventory: Development and psychometric investigation of the client form. *Psychotherapy*, 47, 540–553.

Kerr, M. E. (1981). Family systems theory and therapy. In A. S. Gurman & D. P. Kniskern (Eds.), *Handbook of family therapy* (pp. 226–264). New York: Brunner Mazel.

Kerr, M. E. (1998). Bowen theory and evolutionary theory. *Family Systems*, 4, 119–179.

Kerr, M. E. (2013). The ultra-modern synthesis. *Family Systems*, 9, 133–142.

Kerr, M., & Bowen, M. (1988). *Family evaluation.* New York: Norton Press.

Kivlighan, D. M., Gelso, C. J., Ain, S., Hummel, A. M., & Markin, R. D. (2015). The therapist, the client, and the real relationship: An actor-partner interdependence analysis of treatment outcome. *Journal of Counseling Psychology*, 62, 314–320.

Latts, M. A., & Gelso, C. J. (1995). Countertransference behavior and management with survivors of sexual assault. *Psychotherapy*, 32, 405–415.

Ligiero, D. P., & Gelso, C. J. (2002). Countertransference, attachment, and the working alliance: The therapist's contribution. *Psychotherapy*, 39, 3–11.

Linehan, M. (1993). *Cognitive-behavioral treatment of borderline personality disorder.* New York: Guilford Press.

Lo Coco, G., Gullo, S., Prestano, C., & Gelso, C. J. (2011). Relation of the real relationship and the working alliance to the outcome of brief psychotherapy. *Psychotherapy*, 48, 359–367.

Luborsky, D. (1976). Helping alliance in psychotherapy: The groundwork for a study of their relationship to its outcome. In J. L. Claghorn (Ed.), *Successful psychotherapy* (pp. 92–116). New York: Brunner/Mazel.

Markin, R. D., Kivlighan, D. M., Gelso, C. J., Hummel, A. M., & Spiegel, E. B. (2014). Clients' and therapists' real relationship and session quality in brief therapy: An actor partner interdependence analysis. *Psychotherapy*, 51, 413–423.

Marmarosh, C. L., Gelso, C. J., Markin, R. D., Majors, R., Mallery, C., & Choi, J. (2009). The real relationship in psychotherapy: Relationship to adult attachments, working alliance, transference, and therapy outcome. *Journal of Counseling Psychology*, 56, 337–350.

Martin, D. J., Garske, J. P., & Davis, M. K.. (2000). Relation of the therapeutic alliance with outcome and other variables. *Journal of Consulting and Clinical Psychology*, 68, 438–450.

Meissner, W. W. (1964). Thinking about the family-psychiatric aspects. *Family Process*, 3, 1–40.

Meissner, W. W. (1992). The concept of the therapeutic alliance. *Journal of the American Psychoanalytic Association*, 40, 1059–1087.

Meissner, W. W. (1996a). Empathy in the therapeutic alliance. *Psychoanalytic Inquiry*, 16, 39–53.

Meissner, W. W. (1996b). *The therapeutic alliance.* New Haven, CT: Yale University Press.

Meissner, W. W. (1998). Neutrality, abstinence, and the therapeutic alliance. *Journal of the American Psychoanalytic Association*, 46, 1089–1126.

Meissner, W. W. (1999). Notes on the therapeutic role of the alliance. *The Psychoanalytic Review*, 86, 1–33.

Meissner, W. W. (2000). The many faces of analytic interaction. *Psychoanalytic Psychology*, 17, 512–546.

Meissner, W. W. (2006a). The therapeutic alliance—A proteus in disguise. *Psychotherapy: Theory. Research. Practice. Training*, 43, 264–270.

Meissner, W. W. (2006b). Finding and refining the therapeutic alliance: On thinking in thirds. *The Journal of the American Psychoanalysis & Dynamic Psychiatry*, 34, 651–678.

Meissner, W. W. (2007). Therapeutic alliance: Theme and variations. *Psychoanalytic Psychology*, 34, 231–254.

Menninger, K. A. (1958). *The theory of psychoanalytic technique.* New York: Basic Books.

Moore, S. R., & Gelso, C. J. (2011). Recollections of a secure base in psychotherapy: Considerations of the real relationship. *Psychotherapy*, 48, 368–373.

Noone, R. J., & Papero, D. V. (Eds.). (2015). *The family as an emotional system: An integrative concept for theory, science, and practice.* New York: Lexington Books.

Norcross, J. C. (2002). *Psychotherapy relationships that work.* New York: Oxford University Press.

Papero, D. V. (1990). *Bowen family systems theory.* Boston, MA: Allyn & Bacon.

Rakow, C. M. (September 2007). *Bowen's early research: The foundation of a new theory.* Paper presented to the Postgraduate Program, Bowen Center for the Study for the Family, Washington, DC.

Robinson, L., Berman, J. S., & Neimeyer, R. A. (1990). Psychotherapy for the treatment of depression: A comprehensive review of controlled outcome research. *Psychological Bulletin*, 108, 30–49.

Safran, J., & Muran, J. C. (2000). *Negotiating the therapeutic alliance: A relational treatment guide.* New York: Guilford Press.

Safran, J., & Muran, J. C. (2006). Has the concept of the therapeutic alliance outlives its usefulness? *Psychotherapy: Theory, Research, Practice, Training*, 43, 300–307.

Samstag, L. W. (2006). The working alliance in psychotherapy: An overview of the invited papers in this special section. *Psychotherapy: Theory, Research, Practice, Training*, 43, 258–263.

Shedler, J. (2010). The efficacy of psychodynamic psychotherapy. *American Psychologist*, 65, 98–109.

Shirk, S., Karver, M. S., & Brown, S. (2011). The alliance in child and adolescent psychotherapy. *Psychotherapy*, 48, 17–24.

Smith, M. L., Glass, G. V., & Miller, T. I. (1980). *The benefits of psychotherapy.* Baltimore, MD: Johns Hopkins University Press.

Sterba, R. (1934). The fate of the ego in psychoanalytic therapy. *International Journal of Psychoanalysis*, 9, 363–379.

Strupp, H. H. (1963). The outcome problem in psychotherapy revisited. *Psychotherapy: Theory, Research & Practice*, 1, 1–13.

Titelman, P. (1987). *The therapists own family.* Northvale, NJ: Jason Aronson.

Titelman, P. (1998). *Clinical applications of Bowen family systems theory.* New York: Haworth Press.

Toman, W. (1961). *Family constellation.* New York: Springer.

Wagoner, S. L., Gelso, C. J., Hayes, J. A., & Diemer, R. A. (1991). Countertransference and the reputedly excellent therapist. *Psychotherapy*, 28, 411–421.

Wynne, L. C., Ryckoff, I. M., Fay, J., & Hirsch, S. I. (1958). Pseudomutuality in the family relationships of schizophrenics. *Psychiatry*, 21, 205–220.

Zetzel, E. R. (1956). The concept of transference. *International Journal of Psychoanalysis*, 37, 369–375.

Index